AT
TIMBERLINE

AT
TIMBERLINE
A NATURE GUIDE
TO THE
MOUNTAINS OF THE NORTHEAST

FREDERIC L. STEELE

Illustrations by

Arlene Soule
Cindy House
Robin Brickman

APPALACHIAN MOUNTAIN CLUB
BOSTON, MASSACHUSETTS

AT TIMBERLINE:
A NATURE GUIDE TO THE MOUNTAINS OF THE NORTHEAST

Copyright © 1982 by Appalachian Mountain Club

Printed in the United States of America.

FIRST EDITION

ISBN 0-910146-39-X

Contents

Acknowledgments

Plant lists were furnished by John Glasser, resident naturalist at the AMC huts in the White Mountains, Gerald Merry, naturalist at Baxter State Park, and Peter Zika. Tudor Richards, director of the Audubon Society of New Hampshire, furnished bird lists and reviewed the manuscript on birds. Harry McDade advised on birds and cold-blooded vertebrates, and Howard Nowell of the New Hampshire Fish and Game Department helped with mammals and cold-blooded vertebrates. Those who assisted with the geology section are Professors Charles Burnham and Marland P. Billings of Harvard University, Katherine Fowler Billings, and Richard P. Tollo, University of North Carolina. Kathy Cook typed the manuscript, correcting many errors in the sheets I furnished her.

At Timberline displays the work of several talented artists. Original plant illustrations were drawn by Arlene Soule, with additional illustrations from the *AMC Field Guide to Mountain Flowers;* bird illustrations are by Cindy House; and mammals and cold-blooded vertebrates were drawn by Robin Brickman.

This guide was authorized by Arlyn Powell, former Director of Publications at the AMC. It would not have been possible without his advice and encouragement. Others at the AMC who ushered the book to publication include Sally Greene Carrel, Director of Publications; Jeri Kane, editorial; and Michael Cirone and Betsey Tryon, production.

Introduction

In 1964 the Appalachian Mountain Club published the *AMC Field Guide to Mountain Flowers of New England*. This was essentially an alpine guide and included all plants (wildflowers, trees, shrubs, ferns, and grasses) occurring above 4000 feet and in the alpine zones of New England and New York.

There are many colorful and interesting plants that occur along trails at lower elevations than 4000 feet. This guide attempts to include all the plants that a hiker might see starting at an elevation of approximately 2000 feet. The emphasis is on woodland plants — not those of fields, roadsides, or parking areas. Some have been omitted either because they are unlikely to be seen or because only minor differences distinguish them from listed ones. All plants known to occur in the alpine zone are included.

Animals are also of interest to the alpine naturalist albeit not as easily observed as plants. This guide describes New England's birds, mammals, and cold-blooded vertebrates, and includes some natural history for many of them.

Names of animals and birds are quite well standardized, although in recent years the names of some birds have been changed. Plants, on the other hand, often have two or more common names, or, at the other end of the spectrum, no recognized common names. In the latter case, names that seem appropriate have been assigned.

There are three major life zones in the mountains related to elevation and, to some extent, to wind exposure. At the bottom is the hardwood forest with beech, yellow birch, white birch, and sugar maple predominant. Many flowers and birds are found primarily in this zone. Farther up is the coniferous forest with fir balsam and red spruce predominant. Different birds and flowers will be found here, but not as many species as in the hardwood forest.

Near the summits of the higher mountains is the alpine zone where trees are stunted or absent. Although this is a harsh zone with low temperatures, high winds, and a short growing season, a number of lowland plants flourish here along with the true arctic alpines. Various birds occur in or near the alpine zone but all of these can be found in lower mountains and sometimes in northern lowland woods. A few shrews and mice are restricted to the alpine zone, but these are seldom seen. Caribou, once abundant on the plateau of Katahdin, have long since disappeared.

A number of lower mountains have bare summits with areas suggestive of the alpine zone. Interesting plants characteristic of high elevations may be found here, but rarely the true arctic alpine species.

Each description indicates the elevation at which the plant or animal is most likely to be seen. Low refers to the zone at the bottom of the mountain up to 3000 feet; medium to the zone from 3000 to 4000 feet; and high to elevations near the top or up to the edge of the alpine zone, the border of which varies from 4500 to 5000 feet. The headwalls of the ravines on Washington and of the basins in Katahdin are in the alpine zone. The Krummholz, home of dwarf birches and willows, is the low, thick balsam forest found in sheltered parts of the alpine zone.

When you are in the mountains, keep good conservation practices in mind. Picking flowers in the alpine regions of Washington and Katahdin is not allowed. In the past, populations of some of the rare species were greatly reduced by excessive picking or collecting. Trampling can also destroy plants or alter the soil composition they require. In the alpine zone, the recommended procedure is to stay on the trail, especially in areas where there is vegetation.

If a plant is abundant in the woodlands, it does no harm to pick a few. Trailside flowers should be left for all to enjoy. While some mountain plants have edible leaves or roots, others are poisonous. Unless you are certain of identification, don't assume that anything can be safely eaten.

Selected References

Birds of North America, Robbins et. al., Golden Press, New York, NY.

Newcomb's Wildflower Guide, Newcomb, Little, Brown, Boston, MA.

Trees and Shrubs of Northern New England, Steele and Hodgdon, Society for the Protection of New Hampshire Forests, Concord, NH.

The Peterson Field Guide Series, Houghton Mifflin, Boston, MA.

    A Field Guide to the Birds, Peterson.

    A Field Guide to the Mammals, Burt and Grossenheider.

    A Field Guide to Animal Tracks, Murie.

    A Field Guide to Reptiles and Amphibians of the United States and Canada East of the 100th Meridian, Conant.

    A Field Guide to Wildflowers of Northeastern and North-central North America, Peterson and McKenny.

    A Field Guide to Trees and Shrubs (Northeastern and Central North America), Petrides.

    A Field Guide to the Ferns and Their Related Families of Northeastern and Central North America, Cobb.

How To Use This Book

This book, to our knowledge, is the first to gather between two covers all the information you will need to identify the flora and fauna of New England's mountainsides — an undertaking that previously required more than several guidebooks and as many added pounds in the hiker's backpack.

At Timberline is divided into two main sections: plants and animals. Plants includes wildflowers, trees and shrubs, ferns and fern allies, and grasses and grasslike plants. Animals includes birds, mammals, and cold-blooded vertebrates.

This guide presents a nontechnical, visual approach for the layman. Nearly all of more than five hundred plants and animals are illustrated, and the accompanying text covers distinguishing characteristics and habitat. Botanical terms have been included in plant descriptions only when such technical information aids in identification. Definitions of terms and labeled illustrations can be found in the chapter openings.

The field-guide format has also been adapted to identify and illustrate some common geological features of New England's mountains, for you will invariably notice and wonder about the rich variety of rock and land formations you see along the trail.

Geology

New England's mountains look the way they do because of forces that built them and forces that eroded them. Mountain-building happens on a physical scale so vast that it is extremely difficult to imagine. It is also a slow process — some of the bedrock exposed in Vermont's Green Mountains was formed a billion years ago. Although many geologic features associated with mountain-building are complex and difficult for the non-geologist to decipher, some can easily be identified by an untrained observer, and so they have been included.

The most obvious geologic features in New England's mountains are glacial in origin, and therefore much more recent than the last great mountain-building episode, which occurred 300 to 350 million years ago. Ice from last glaciation finished melting only about 12,000 years ago, a geologic eyeblink.

The great continental ice sheets and smaller alpine glaciers that formed in mountain valleys did not build or destroy mountains. They sculpted the landscape and modified its contours. Their erosive effects are very visible, and relationships between glacial action and what we see are easy to understand. Most of the geologic features described below are, therefore, glacial.

Erosion continues, on a lesser scale to be sure than that resulting from the great ice sheets, and so a few examples of alterations to mountain surfaces that are taking place now are included. The overall progression is from great to small changes — from mountain-building to mountain landslides.

Because they are complex and because better sources are readily available, there has been no attempt to describe rocks and the minerals that rocks are made of. Those interested in identifying the rocks that they see should consult *A Field Guide to Rocks and Minerals* by Frederick H. Pough, listed in the further reading references below.

Further Reading

All of these references are appropriate for the general reader who lacks technical knowledge, but nonetheless wishes to know more.

Jorgensen, Neil. *A Guide to New England's Landscape* (Pequot Press: Chester, Connecticut, 1977). Geography, geology, and botany of New England explained in nontechnical terms. Excellent illustrations, annotated bibliographies, and site directions for viewing New England's natural phenomena.

McPhee, John. *Basin and Range* (Farrar, Straus, Giroux: New York, 1981). The best resource for understanding something about geology without being a geologist.

Pough, Frederick H. *A Field Guide to Rocks and Minerals* (Houghton Mifflin Company: Boston, Massachusetts, 1976). Well-illustrated, written for amateurs. Part of the Peterson Field Guide series.

Thomson, Betty Flanders. *The Changing Face of New England* (Houghton Mifflin Company: Boston, Massachusetts, 1977). How geologic and geographic factors shaped the New England we know today.

To obtain publications with more detailed information about the geology of a particular location, write to

New Hampshire Department of Resources and Economic
   Development
Maine Geological Survey
Vermont Geological Survey
U.S. Geological Survey (for quadrangle maps).

GEOLOGY

Geologic Features Associated with Mountain-Building

BEDROCK

If one imagines the earth's crust as a two-layer cake, bedrock is the solid, unbroken bottom layer, and soil is the unconsolidated top layer. Bedrock is exposed in road cuts, in stream beds, and in the mountains. Mountains were once flat-lying bedrock. Tremendous forces in the earth's crust squeezed the rock together until it buckled upward to form mountain ranges.

Some of the oldest exposed bedrock in New England is in the Green Mountains, from the area north of Chittendon Reservoir, near Holden, Vermont, to the Massachusetts border, approximately 90 miles south. (The Long Trail and the Appalachian Trail coincide for much of this distance.) Bedrock exposed in this section, which is often called the main range of the Green Mountains, is believed to be at least one billion years old.

Exposed bedrock, Swift River, NH (M. Gawecki)

ROCK FOLD

Forces in the earth's crust created such heat and pressure that solid bedrock became plastic and bent.

Above, folded rock near Auto Road to summit, Mt. Washington, NH (M. Gawecki); Below, folded rock in cliff wall west of Mt. Monadnock summit, Jaffey, NH (R. Tollo)

DIKE

A band of rock of varying width that cuts across the structure of the bedrock that surrounds it. Dikes are often different in color and texture from surrounding bedrock. Basalt dikes, common in New England, are smooth, fine-grained, dark rock. Granite dikes are light in color

When forces in the earth's crust pull the bedrock apart, creating deep fissures which penetrate to the molten material or magma deep in the earth's crust, the magma invades these cracks. When it solidifies before it reaches the earth's surface, a dike forms. If the magma reaches the surface still molten, a volcano or a lava flow forms.

Eroding dike, Swift River, NH (M. Gawecki)

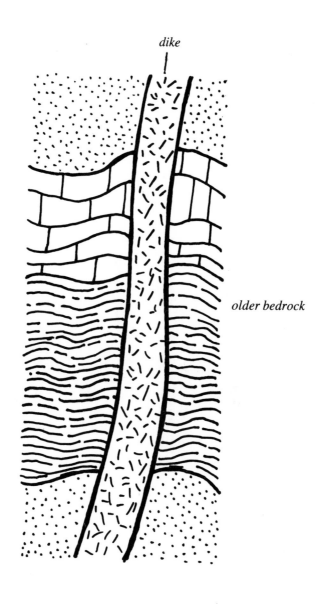

dike

older bedrock

Diagrammatic Representation of a Dike

FLUME

In some cases, basalt dikes are less resistant to erosion than the bedrock which surrounds them. If water flows over its surface, a dike may erode to form a flume — a narrow gorge with steep parallel sides.

The Flume, Franconia Notch, NH (AMC Collection)

MONADNOCK

Isolated hill or mountain that rises above a relatively level plain. The term was generalized from Mount Monadnock in southern New Hampshire.

Continued widespread erosion over millions of years may modify a mountainous landscape and reduce it to an almost-level plain. Monadnocks are remnants of an older landscape. They were more resistant to erosion than the bedrock that formerly surrounded them.

monadnock   *nearly level plain*

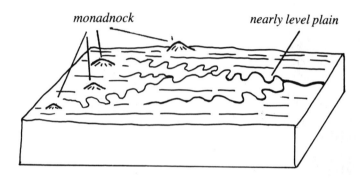

Pack Monadnock, near Peterborough, NH (F. Endicott)

Geologic Features Associated with Glaciation

CIRQUE

A depression in a mountainside that resembles a giant bowl with a piece broken out of it in the downslope direction. It has very steep side walls, a cliff-like back wall, and a rounded bottom, where there is often a small lake, or tarn.

Cirques were the birthplaces of valley glaciers. About two million years ago, in response to a global lowering of temperature and perhaps to increased local precipitation, snow began to accumulate in many elevated mountain areas. With continued accumulation, the snow compacted to ice and — propelled by its own weight — began to flow downward, following the path of mountain valleys. When the top edge of a valley glacier melted on sunny days, the meltwater seeped into cracks in the mountain rock, froze, expanded, and eventually loosened large blocks of rock. With repeated melting and freezing, the valley glacier eventually hollowed out a cirque and, in its downward course, carried away the blocks of rock it had quarried.

Glacial cirque: Tuckerman Ravine, Mt. Washington, NH (W. Pote)

KNIFE EDGE

A narrow ridge from which one can sometimes straddle opposite sides of a mountain. Created when a valley glacier quarried nearly through a steep mountain flank or when two adjacent cirques formed on either side of a mountain. The narrow ridge in the latter case is called an *arete*.

Knife edge, overlooking South Basin, Mt. Katahdin, ME (W. Thompson)

CLIFF AND TALUS

A high steep rock face with a sloping pile of loose boulders and rock fragments of all sizes at its foot.

As the continental ice sheets moved north to south over the mountains, they smoothed, streamlined, and scoured but did not alter basic contours on the north sides. On the southern sides, they tore off chunks of rock, often leaving a sheer, steep face. In post-glacial times, water has seeped into cracks, or joints, in the cliff faces, frozen, expanded, and eventually loosened large blocks of rock, which break away to form the talus below. The cliff known as the Old Man of the Mountain in Franconia Notch, New Hampshire, has been artificially reinforced several times to assure that this landmark retains its recognizable face.

Old Man of the Mountain, Franconia Notch, NH (C. T. Bodwell)

Talus near summit of Mt. Washington, NH (D. Hoyt)

ROCHES MOUTONNEES

Elongate ledges with smooth, gently sloping northern faces and jagged, steep southern faces. Also known as sheepback rocks.

Roches moutonnées were created when the continental ice sheets flowed over knob-shaped bodies of bedrock, froze to blocks of rock and tore them off in the "downstream" or southward direction. The smooth northern faces on many New England roches moutonnees were polished by rock flour, extremely fine-grained rock debris adhering to the ice sheets that passed over them.

Above, roches moutonnees near Lakes of the Clouds, Mt. Washington, NH. Ice flowed from left to right (George Bellerose); below, a much larger roche moutonnee, Mt. Monroe, NH. Ice flowed in direction of slope, from right foreground toward left center peaks (D. Smith)

STRIAE

Regular grooves or scratches in bedrock, usually in parallel sets, that indicate the directional orientation of glaciers that flowed over it.

The continental ice sheets scraped the landscape, picking up all manner of debris, including large hard rocks, as they flowed southward. Under the enormous pressure that thousands of feet of ice bearing down upon them created, rocks on the bottom of the glaciers gouged exposed bedrock as the ice passed over. Striae and glacial till (see below) on the top are evidence that the continental ice sheet overrode Mount Washington and, therefore, that the ice was at one time several thousand feet thick.

Glacial striae, Tuckerman Ravine, Mount Washington, NH (W. Thompson)

GEOLOGY

U-SHAPED VALLEY

Steep-sided valley with a slightly rounded floor.

The continental ice sheet scoured out the bottoms of sharp, V-shaped mountain valleys that had been created by stream erosion, softening them to U-shapes.

Aerial view of U-shaped valley, Crawford Notch, NH (G.E. Campbell)

ERRATIC

A boulder which the ice sheet picked up and transported. When the ice melted, the boulder was dropped, sometimes at a considerable distance from its original location. Erratics are usually rock of a different composition than the bedrock in the immediate area where they were deposited.

Glacial Erratic, South Bubble Mtn., Acadia National Park, ME (R. Tollo)

GLACIAL LAKE

Body of water that formed due to changes in the landscape caused by glaciation.

Glaciers scooped basins out of bedrock or deposited sand, gravel, boulders, clay, and other debris to dam valleys, which then filled with water. Nearly all of New England's natural lakes and ponds exist because of glacial effects. Another kind of basin that the ice sheets created is called a kettlehole. A massive piece of ice detached from the melting glacier, was buried in gravel and debris carried by meltwater streaming from the glacier, then melted itself, leaving a depression. Kettleholes are common throughout New England in the soils deposited in valleys by the receding glaciers.

How Kettleholes Formed

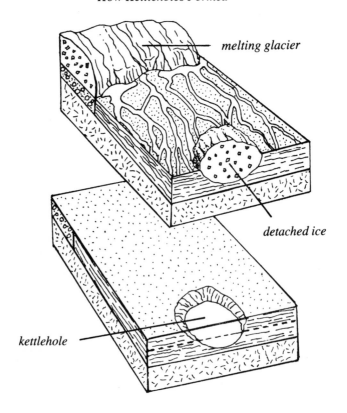

melting glacier

detached ice

kettlehole

Glacial lakes: Lakes of the Clouds, Mt. Washington, NH (C. Robinson)

TILL

A jumbled mixture of sand, clay and different-sized rocks deposited by the ice sheet.

Much of New England's subsoil is till, popularly known as hardpan. Till can easily be seen in the banks of mountain streams.

Glacial till off roadside, Route 113 near Madison, NH (M. Gawecki)

Geologic Features Associated with Nonglacial Erosion

POTHOLE

A depression worn in stream bedrock at falls or rapids. The strong current swirls stones, sand, and gravel to create a cylindrical hollow, deeper than it is wide. These abrasive materials are trapped in the hollow and continue to enlarge it. Potholes are usually shallow, but on occasion they can be six to eight feet deep.

Potholes, Diana's Bath, North Conway, NH (M. Gawecki)

SLIDE

The bare rock exposed when a landslide takes place.

After heavy rain, the soil on steep mountain slopes becomes saturated and slides into the valley below, taking trees and loose rocks with it. Areas bared by landslides may need up to a hundred years to revegetate.

Landslides, Willey Range, Crawford Notch, NH (M. Gawecki)

SPLIT ROCKS

Angular chunks of rock of various sizes, usually more common at higher elevations, where freeze-thaw cycles are more frequent.

All rock has a tendency to split along parallel planes, called joints. Water continues to fill these cracks, freeze, expand, and in the end, split the bedrock.

Split rocks on Boott Spur, Presidential Range, NH (H. Orne)

Wildflowers

This section describes herbs, or what are generally known as wildflowers. An attempt has been made to include all wildflowers that will be found along mountain trails from low elevations through the alpine zone. Weedy flowers of parking areas, roadsides, and building sites — most of which are of European origin — are not included. These can be found in any of several popular guides, though it should be noted that these guides do not include some of the rarer alpine flowers.

You will find some flowering plants in the section on shrubs. Shrubs have woody stems; wildflowers do not. This distinction is not always readily apparent, so it may be necessary to look in both sections for some flowering plants.

Organization

Wildflowers are formally classified by families. But because the distinctions between families are technical ones that will not concern us in this field guide, it is more practical to order the wildflowers primarily by color and, when useful, by structural characteristics easily observed in the field.

At the outset, though, a word of caution is in order. Color distinctions are not always easy to make. Reddish-brown flowers should be looked for in both the red and brown sections. Some flowers listed in the white section have pink stripes or may prove to be pale yellow on close examination. Others are colors that are difficult to describe, or a flower may occasionally take another color. For example, lady's slippers are usually pink, but white forms are fairly common in the mountains. Likewise, some white flowers occasionally take pink forms. When in doubt, look for the flower in several likely sections.

Particularly in the case of the largest color group, the white flowers, it is useful to subdivide the group. This section is broken down according to whether the flower is **regular**, petals of the same size and shape, or **irregular**, petals of different shapes, such as the violet. Regular flowers are further distinguished by number of petals and arrangement of leaves.

Leaves may be **opposite**, directly opposite each other on the stem, or **alternate**, borne singly along the stem at different levels. Sometimes they are in **whorls,** with three or more leaves arising from the same point on the stem, or **basal**, arising from the base of the stem. A **compound** leaf is a single leaf that is divided into separate leaflike segments, or leaflets.

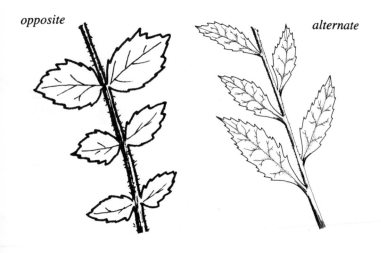

opposite   *alternate*

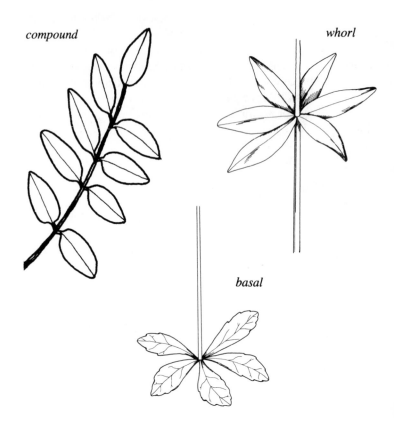

compound

whorl

basal

Botanical Terms

Some entries refer to specific parts of a flower when these parts serve to distinguish the flower from others. An illustration of the parts of a flower is provided.

In general, the flower is the reproductive part of the plant. It consists of the male **stamen**, which encompasses the pollen-carrying **anther**, and the female **pistil**, at the base of which is the **ovary**. The **petals**, collectively called the **corolla**, are surrounded by an outer circle of floral parts called the **calyx**, whose green leaflike **sepals** enclose the flower in bud.

Flowers cannot develop seeds unless pollination occurs, which involves the transfer of pollen to the pistil, usually from one flower to another. The pollen fertilizes **ovules** in the ovary, where they develop into seeds. The seeds are encased in **fruit**, whose many forms include the pod, acorn, and sweet pulp of an apple or blueberry.

Bees often aid in pollination as they gather nectar to make honey. The odd shapes of some flowers expressly ensure that pollen from the anthers will brush off on bees.

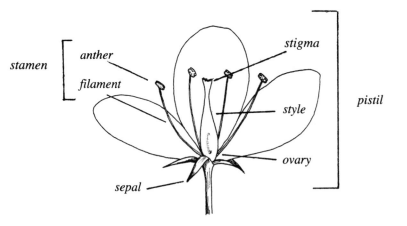

Entries

Most people turn to the illustrations first in order to identify an unfamiliar wildflower. The text includes other helpful data: size; descriptions of leaves, fruits and berries; flowers and flowering season; and habitat and elevation.

Flowers Yellow or Straw-Colored   *Parts in 3's or 6's*

YELLOW-EYED GRASS   *Xyris montana*

Leaves grasslike, all at base, flowers yellow ¼ **inch wide, 3 petals in a scaly head.** Occasional in bogs and on sandy shores of ponds at low elevations. Flowers July to Sept.

WILD OAT   *Uvularia sessilifolia*
or BELLWORT

Plant up to 1 foot high, leaves near the top of the stem with pale undersides, 1 or 2 pale yellow or straw-colored flowers with 6 parts, **bell-shaped and hanging,** fruit a triangular pod. Common in hardwoods at low elevations. Flowers late April to May. After flowering, becomes taller and stem forks with pod hanging beneath.

CANADA LILY   *Lilium canadense*

Stem 2 to 4 feet tall, leaves in several whorls, **1 or more nodding flowers with 6 parts at the top of the stem,** orange or yellow. Occasional in wet woods or openings on lower slopes. Flowers mid-June to mid-Aug.

DOGTOOTH VIOLET   *Erythronium americanum*
or TROUT LILY

Stem up to 1 foot high, **2 mottled leaves at the base,** 1 nodding yellow flower with 6 parts at the top. Occasional in hardwoods at low elevations. Flowers in May. In spite of the name this is not a violet. The mottled leaves are colored like a trout.

CLINTONIA   *Clintonia borealis*

Stem about 1 foot high, 2 to 4 leaves at the base, **2 to 8 yellow flowers with 6 parts at the top of the stem,** fruit a blue berry. Common in woods and open areas at all elevations and in alpine meadows. Flowers in May in the lowlands, June to Aug. at high elevations. It is inadvisable to eat the berry in great quantities.

SOLOMON'S SEAL   *Polygonatum biflorum*

Stem 1 to 2 feet high, leaves pale beneath, flowers greenish-yellow with 6 parts, tubular and **hanging under the stem,** fruit a blue-black berry. Frequent in hardwoods at low elevations. Flowers May, June. A round scar on the root is the "seal."

yellow-eyed grass

wild oat

dogtooth violet

Canada lily

clintonia

Solomon's seal

37

INDIAN CUCUMBER   *Medeola virginiana*

Stem up to 3 feet high, **leaves in 2 whorls, one near the middle of the stem, the other at the top,** flowers greenish-yellow with 6 parts, hanging down under the top leaves, fruit a dark purple berry. Frequent in hardwoods at low elevations. Flowers May, June. The root has a flavor of cucumber.

Flowers Yellow or Straw-Colored   *Parts in 4's or 5's*

YELLOW POND LILY   *Nuphar variegatum*
or COW LILY

Leaves 4 to 12 inches long, **usually floating in water,** flowers with 5 or 6 yellow sepals and numerous small petals. Frequent near the edges of ponds at low elevations. Flowers May to Sept. Muskrats dig up the large root for food.

NORTHERN WINTER CRESS   *Barbarea orthoceras*

Flowers with **4 pale yellow petals.** Once found in a ravine on Washington, more common in eastern Canada. Flowers June to Aug.

YELLOW MOUNTAIN SAXIFRAGE   *Saxifraga aizoides*

Stem up to 5 inches tall, **basal leaves fleshy and forming loose mats,** 1 to 20 flowers in a cluster, yellow, often red-dotted. Rare on cliffs in Vermont at low elevations. Flowers June to Sept.

SIBBALDIA   *Sibbaldia procumbens*

Low tufted plant with compound leaves divided into 3 leaflets, resembling three-toothed cinquefoil but **slightly hairy, flower small, yellow** with 5 petals. Rare in a ravine on Washington, widespread in the Arctic. Flowers in July. Although there are only a few colonies on Washington, they are far from any trails and not likely to be exterminated.

DWARF CINQUEFOIL   *Potentilla Robbinsiana*

Dwarf tufted plant about 1 inch high, leaves compound with 3 leaflets, flowers yellow with 5 petals about ¼ inch across. Rare on Washington, occuring in one small barren area. Flowers in June. This plant is endemic to New Hampshire alone. It formerly grew on Mt. Lafayette but has since been exterminated, probably unintentionally trampled by hikers.

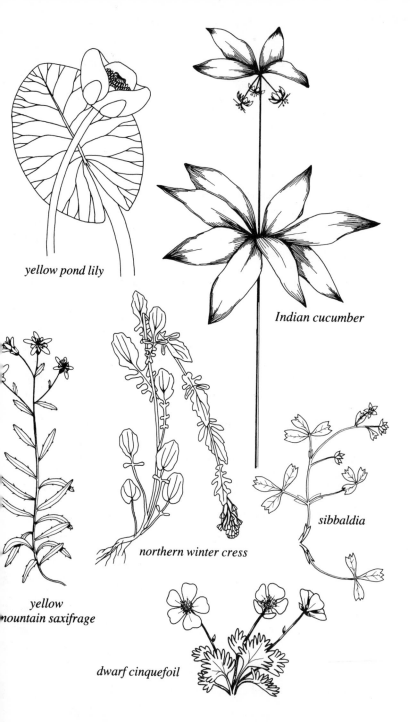

yellow pond lily

Indian cucumber

northern winter cress

sibbaldia

yellow
mountain saxifrage

dwarf cinquefoil

ROUGH CINQUEFOIL   *Potentilla norvegica*

Stem up to 1 foot high covered with spreading hairs, leaves compound with 3 leaflets, flowers yellow with 5 petals, **about ¼ inch across, surrounded by prominent leafy sepals.** Occasional in dry places in alpine ravines and on summits, and in open areas of lower mountains.

MOUNTAIN AVENS   *Geum Peckii*

Leaves at the base of the stem nearly round, flowers yellow with 5 petals and nearly round, **resembling a buttercup.** Common in the alpine area of the Presidential Range, frequent in damp areas and on wet cliffs at lower elevations west to the Franconias and Cannon Mountain. Flowers June to Sept. Although the plant is common in the White Mountains, it does not occur anywhere else in the world except on Brier Island, Nova Scotia.

LARGE-LEAVED AVENS   *Geum macrophyllum*

Plant up to 3 feet high, **basal leaf round, on a stem 2 to 4 inches long with small leaflets along the stem,** smaller leaves on the main stem, flowers yellow with 5 petals about ½ inch across. Occasional in damp thickets and openings at low and medium elevations. Flowers June to Aug.

EARLY YELLOW VIOLET   *Viola rotundifolia*

Low plant up to 2 inches high, **leaves all at the base of the stem, heart-shaped.** Flowers yellow with 5 petals and a typical violet shape. Common in hardwoods at low elevations. Flowers from late April to mid-May. This is one of the earliest of the spring flowers.

NORTHERN ST. JOHNSWORT   *Hypericum boreale*

Low plant up to 1 foot high, leaves about ½ inch wide, **numerous small yellow flowers less than ¼ inch across** with 5 petals. Occasional in wet places or on edges of ponds at low elevations. Flowers July, Aug. Other St. Johnsworts found in similar locations.

PINESAP   *Monotropa hypopithys*

Up to 6 inches high, root parasite with **no green leaves,** plant and flowers **tawny or yellowish,** flowers with 5 petals. Occasional in woods at low elevations. Flowers June to Sept. The leaves are replaced by scales and the plant gets its nourishment from roots of other plants or dead vegetable matter.

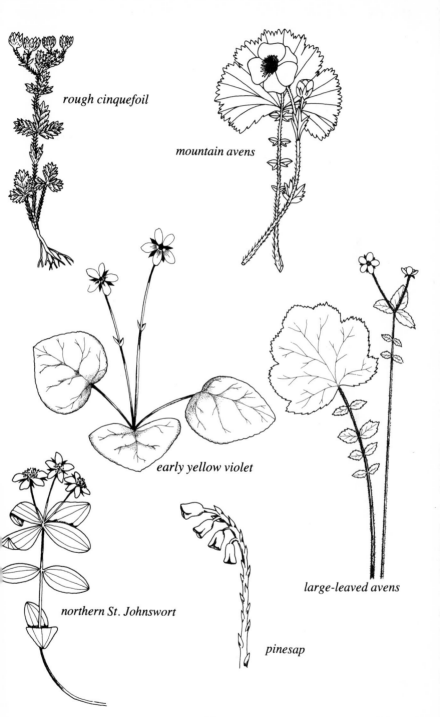

rough cinquefoil

mountain avens

early yellow violet

large-leaved avens

northern St. Johnswort

pinesap

YELLOW LOOSESTRIFE   *Lysimachia terrestris*

Plant up to 3 feet tall, **leaves opposite,** flowers with 5 narrow yellow petals with **dark streaks or dots.** Frequent in open woods and wet areas at low elevations. Flowers July, Aug.

FRINGED LOOSESTRIFE   *Lysimachia ciliata*

Plant up to 3 feet high, **leaves opposite,** flowers with 5 yellow petals, **nearly round and slightly toothed at the end.** Occasional in open woods mostly at low elevations. Flowers July, Aug.

PAINTED CUP   *Castilleja septentrionalis*

Plant up to 2 feet high, flowers greenish or yellowish, **2-lipped, crowded together in a spike.** Occasional in moist or gravelly areas of alpine ravines on the Presidential Range and Katahdin, more common in eastern Canada. Flowers July, Aug.

YELLOW RATTLE   *Rhinanthus Crista-galli*

Plant up to 1 foot high, flowers yellow, **2-lipped, calyx bladder-like and inflated with fruit.** Rare in moist alpine areas, more common in lowlands north of the mountains. Flowers June to Sept.

HORNED BLADDERWORT   *Utricularia cornuta*

Stem erect up to 8 inches high with **no leaves,** flowers yellow, **2-lipped with a conspicuous spur projecting from the base.** Occasional in bogs and on muddy shores of ponds at low and medium elevations. Flowers June to Aug.

WILD LETTUCE   *Lactuca canadensis*

Flowers yellow. Plant similar to the lettuce described in the blue section and found in similar locales.

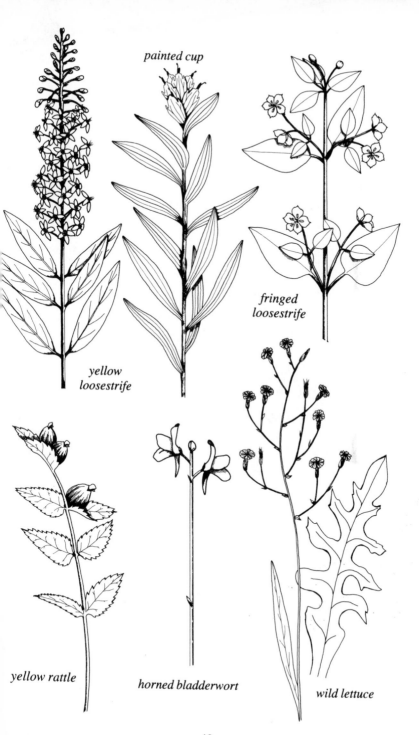

painted cup

fringed
loosestrife

yellow
loosestrife

yellow rattle

horned bladderwort

wild lettuce

43

GOLDENRODS

Members of the composite family, goldenrods have many small yellow flowers growing together in heads. What appear to be petals surrounding the heads are actually ray flowers, each one consisting of five petals fused together. Differentiation is difficult in the lowlands but easier in the mountains where there are fewer species.

ALPINE GOLDENROD   *Solidago Cutleri*

Low plant 3 to 10 inches high, 2 to 7 leaves on stem, not much smaller than the basal leaves, heads in a rather compact cluster. Common in alpine areas of Katahdin, Presidential Range, and Adirondacks. Flowers June to early Sept. Any low goldenrod in the alpine zone is likely to be this species.

MOUNTAIN GOLDENROD   *Solidago Randii*

Similar to alpine goldenrod but **taller, up to 2 feet high, 5 to 20 leaves on the stem** which are smaller than the basal leaves. Common on open ledges at low elevations and on rocky mountain summits, occasional in the alpine zone. Flowers June to Sept. Mountain and alpine goldenrods intergrade to some extent, making identification impossible.

LARGE-LEAVED GOLDENROD   *Solidago macrophylla*

Up to 3 feet tall, **basal leaves large and broad,** from 2 to 5 inches long, **flower heads large,** up to ½ inch high. Common in the woods at all elevations, frequent in the alpine zone in grassy areas in the Krummholz. Flowers July to Sept. In the alpine zone this plant tends to have larger flower heads.

BOG GOLDENROD   *Solidago Purshii*

Plant 1 to 4 feet high, **lower leaves narrow and rather fleshy,** flowering heads in a loose wandlike spike. Occasional in bogs at low and medium elevations. Flowers July to Sept.

ROUGH-STEMMED GOLDENROD   *Solidago rugosa*

Up to 4 feet high, **leaves rough, stem hairy, flowers in curved one-sided clusters.** Common in woods and open areas at low elevations. Flowers July to Sept.

alpine goldenrod

large-leaved goldenrod

mountain goldenrod

bog goldenrod

rough-stemmed goldenrod

45

Flowers Pink, Purple or Blue

This section describes first pink, then purple, then blue flowers, with the transitional pinkish-purple and blue-violet varieties blended in between them.

FIREWEED   *Epilobium angustifolium*

Plant up to 6 feet high, very leafy, flowers with 4 petals, pink or magenta in a **large loose spike 6 to 18 inches long.** Frequent in open areas at low elevations, less common to high elevations and the alpine area. Flowers July, Aug. It gets its name from the fact that it often grows in areas of recent fires.

PINK CORYDALIS   *Corydalis sempervirens*

Plant up to 2 feet tall, **leaves delicate, divided, pale green,** flowers long and narrow, pink with a yellow tip. Frequent on ledges or in dry areas at low elevations. Flowers June to Sept. This plant often grows on ledges where there is little water; in dry seasons it wilts and shrivels.

LADY'S SLIPPER   *Cypripedium acaule*

Plant about 1 foot high with **2 large leaves at the base of the stem, flowers pink with a distinct shape suggesting a shoe.** Occasional in dry woods at low elevations. Flowers in June. In the mountains a white form is quite common. The peculiar shape of the flower aids in pollination by bees.

SWEET BROOM   *Hedysarum alpinum*

Resembles milk vetch but flowers pink to magenta **more than ½ inch long.** Occasional in similar locales. Flowers June to Aug. This plant tends to be bigger than milk vetch but the two species are best distinguished by differences in the pods.

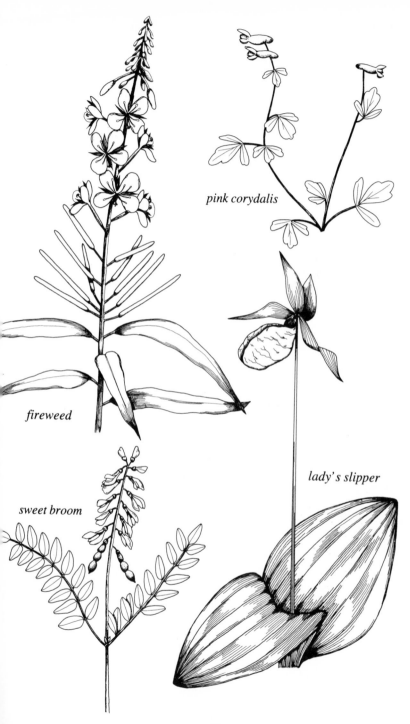

pink corydalis

fireweed

sweet broom

lady's slipper

SPRING BEAUTY   *Claytonia caroliniana*

Delicate plant about 3 inches high with **2 succulent leaves near the middle of the stem,** flowers with 5 petals white or pink with **deeper pink stripes.** Occasional in rich hardwoods at low and medium elevations, rare in alpine meadows. Flowers in May in the lowlands, in June in the alpine region. The tuber is edible, but the plant should not be dug up for this purpose unless there are large masses of it.

TWINFLOWER   *Linnaea borealis*

Trailing plant with **opposite leaves obscurely toothed** about ½ inch long, flowers pink, **funnel-shaped, in pairs.** Frequent on mountain slopes in woods, extending up to the krummholz in the alpine area. Flowers June to Aug. It is named after Linnaeus, a Swedish botanist who is considered the father of modern botany.

JOE-PYE WEED   *Eupatorium maculatum*

Plant up to 6 feet high, **leaves in whorls of 4's or 5's,** stem finely spotted with purple, flowers pinkish-purple in flat-topped clusters. Frequent in thickets or wet places at low elevations. Flowers mid-July to Sept.

MAYFLOWER   *Epigaea repens*
or TRAILING ARBUTUS

This plant has pale pink or white flowers. It is described in the white section.

ALPINE AZALEA   *Loiseleuria procumbens*

A dwarf alpine shrub with pink flowers that is described in the shrub section.

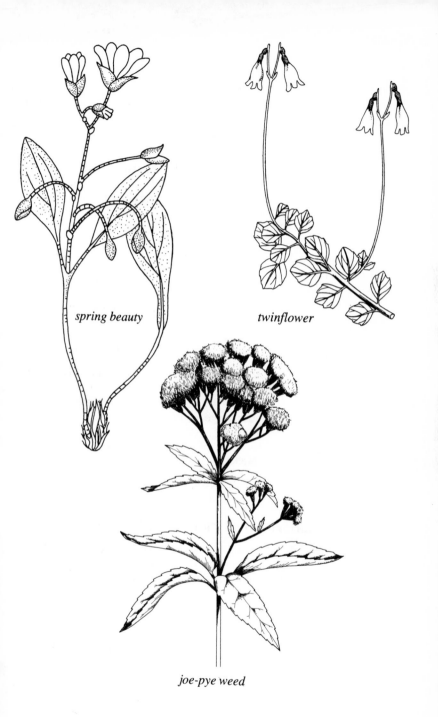

spring beauty

twinflower

joe-pye weed

49

WILLOW HERBS

These plants have small pinkish flowers with 4 petals notched at the tip. The seed pods are long and have many seeds with silky hairs.

MARSH WILLOW HERB *Epilobium palustre*

Low plant 4 to 10 inches high, **leaves narrow without teeth, margins usually inrolled,** flowers with 4 petals less than ¼ inch across, violet to pink or nearly white. Occasional in boggy places at low elevations, becoming more common in wet places in alpine ravines and alpine areas. Flowers July, Aug.

PURPLE-LEAVED WILLOW HERB *Epilobium coloratum*

Stem up to 3 feet high, often branched, **leaves veiny, irregularly toothed,** lower flower clusters **much branched,** flowers pink with 4 petals. Frequent in open areas and wet places at low elevations. Flowers July to Oct.

ALPINE WILLOW HERB *Epilobium Hornemanni*

Plant 6 to 12 inches high, **tufted, with several plants in a clump,** leaves with **shallow, widely separated teeth,** flowers with 4 petals **lilac or pink.** Frequent in wet places in ravines and alpine areas of Katahdin, Presidential Range, and Adirondacks, also in the Arctic. Flowers mid-June to Aug.

ALPINE WILLOW HERB *Epilobium alpinum*

Closely resembles the preceding but leaves firmer and **flowers nearly white.** Occurs in similar locales.

PIMPERNEL WILLOW HERB *Epilobium anagallidifolium*

Resembles the 2 preceding species, dwarf, up to 6 inches high, **stem curving,** flowers pink or purple. Rare in wet places on Katahdin, more common in the mountains of eastern Canada. Flowers July, Aug.

pimpernel willow herb

marsh willow herb

alpine willow herbs

purple-leaved willow herb

51

PURPLE TWISTED STALK   *Streptopus roseus*

1 to 2 feet tall, **stem forking,** leaves without stalks seated directly on the stem, flowers rose-pink or purple with **6 recurved parts, hanging under the stem,** fruit a red berry. Frequent in hardwoods mostly at low elevations, also in moist alpine meadows. Flowers May to July. In the alpine area it often intergrades with mountain twisted stalk.

PURPLE SAXIFRAGE   *Saxifrage oppositifolia*

Low matted plant with a stem that is partly woody, **leaves opposite and small, less than ¼ inch long,** flowers with 5 small petals, **showy, purple.** Occasional on cliffs at low elevations in Vermont. Flowers in mid-May. This plant is only in bloom for a week but during that time forms masses of color on cliffs.

ORCHIDS

The flowers are irregular in shape, somewhat resembling the tropical orchids of the flower shops but much smaller. The flowers have 3 petals, with the front one larger and prolonged at the base into a spur. They have purple, green or white flowers, and are described in the appropriate sections.

PURPLE-FRINGED ORCHID   *Habenaria fimbriata*

Plant up to 3 feet high, purple flowers with 3 petals, a **prominently fringed lip, in a showy cluster.** Occasional in wet places at low and medium elevations. Flowers mid-July, Aug. Although the flowers are usually purple they may be paler or almost white. A similar smaller plant is considered by some botanists to be a separate species.

HEART-LEAVED TWAYBLADE   *Listera cordata*

Plant 4 to 10 inches high with **2 opposite leaves in the middle of the stem,** flowers small with 6 parts, purplish to greenish. Rare in mossy woods at low and medium elevations. Flowers mid-June to Aug.

purple twisted stalk

purple saxifrage

heart-leaved twayblade

purple-fringed orchid

53

LARGE CORALROOT   *Corallorhiza maculata*

Stem about 1 foot high with no green leaves, flowers whitish with 6 parts, spotted with red or purple. Occasional in woods at low elevations. Flowers July, Aug. This plant is a saprophyte which, lacking green leaves, derives its nourishment from dead vegetable matter.

BOG ASTER   *Aster nemoralis*

Plant 1 to 2 feet high, leaves not clasping or heart-shaped, **narrow, very numerous, 1 to 2 inches long,** flowers light violet, **head often single** or up to 10 on a plant. Occasional on boggy shores of ponds at low and medium elevations. Flowers Aug., Sept.

MOSS CAMPION   *Silene acaulis*

Dwarf, **forming dense matted tussocks,** leaves small and narrow, **somewhat mosslike,** flowers pale lilac with 5 petals less than ¼ inch across. Rare in the alpine area of Washington, more common in the mountains of eastern Canada. Flowers mid-June to mid-July. Although the flowers are small they are abundant, and the plant makes a good show when in flower.

ROCK CRESS   *Arabis drummondi*

The flowers of this plant are sometimes pale purple. It is described in the white section.

MOUNTAIN HEATH   *Phyllodoce caerulea*

A low alpine shrub with bell-shaped flowers that is described in the shrub section.

LAPLAND ROSEBAY   *Rhododendron lapponicum*

A low alpine shrub with colorful purple flowers that is described in the shrub section.

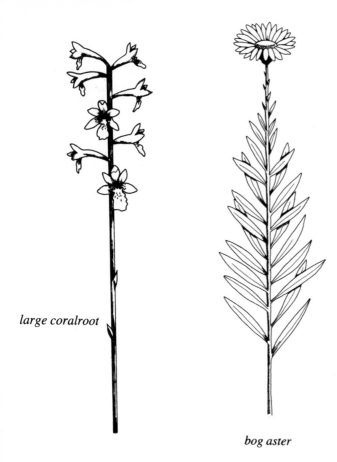

large coralroot

bog aster

moss campion

55

CLOSED GENTIAN   *Gentiana clausa*

Stem 1 to 2 feet tall with **opposite, egg-shaped leaves,** flowers with 5 blue-violet petals **pressed close together at the tip.** Occasional in moist open places at low elevations. Flowers Sept., Oct.

NARROW-LEAVED GENTIAN   *Gentiana linearis*

Similar to the above but with **narrow leaves.** Occasional in bogs or wet places at low elevations. Flowers Aug., Sept. Leaf illustrated with closed gentian.

HAREBELL   *Campanula rotundifolia*
or BLUEBELL

Delicate plant about 8 inches high, **round leaves at the base, narrow leaves on the stem,** flowers violet-blue, **nodding, bell-shaped.** Occasional on cliffs at low elevations, common in alpine areas. Flowers July to Sept. In midsummer this is one of the most colorful flowers in the alpine zone.

AMERICAN BROOKLIME   *Veronica americana*

Plant 6 to 18 inches tall, **leaves opposite** with shallow teeth, flowers blue to lilac with **4 petals, in several loose clusters from the upper part of the stem.** Occasional in wet places at low and medium elevations. Flowers June to Aug.

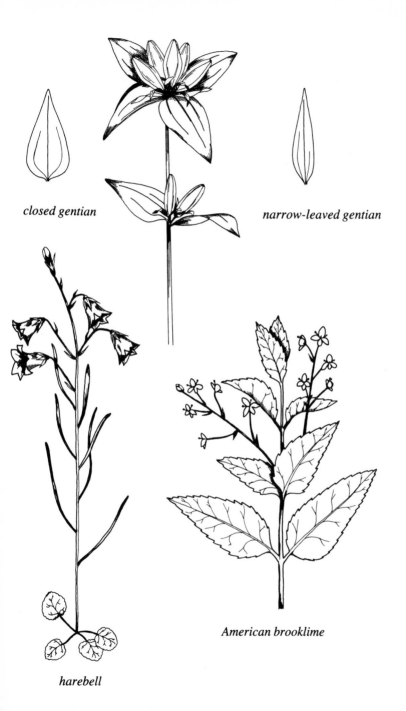

closed gentian

narrow-leaved gentian

American brooklime

harebell

ASTERS

Asters are members of the composite family. Like goldenrods, they have many small flowers packed together in a head and ray flowers that could be mistaken for petals. Asters are difficult to differentiate, but a limited number occur in the mountains. White asters are treated in the section on white flowers.

LARGE-LEAVED ASTER　　　　　　　　*Aster macrophyllus*

Plant up to 4 feet high, **basal leaves large, rough, heart-shaped,** numerous tufts of basal leaves without a flower stalk, flowers violet or pale blue, heads 1 inch or more wide. Common in dry woods and open areas at low and medium elevations. Flowers Aug., Sept.

HEART-LEAVED ASTER　　　　　　　　*Aster cordifolius*

Plant 1 to 3 feet high, lower and middle leaves **heart-shaped with thin stalks,** flowers blue-violet to rose, heads numerous in forking clusters, **rather small, about ½ inch wide.** Common in woods at low elevations. Flowers Aug., Sept.

PURPLE-STEMMED ASTER　　　　　　　*Aster puniceus*

Plant up to 6 feet high, **leaves tapering to a clasping base,** stem stout and hairy, usually reddish, flowers from deep blue to nearly white, heads 1 to 1½ inches across. Common in open woods and wet places at low and medium elevations, occasional in alpine ravines. Flowers Aug., Sept.

MOUNTAIN ASTER　　　　　　　　　　*Aster foliaceus*

Resembles purple-stemmed aster and replaces it in the alpine area. Leaves partly clasping or not clasping, **heads surrounded by numerous rather large leafy parts (bracts).** Frequent in moist or gravelly places in alpine ravines and alpine areas, occasional at low elevations. Flowers Aug., Sept.

ROUGH-LEAVED ASTER　　　　　　　　*Aster radula*

Plant 1 to 3 feet high, leaves not heart-shaped or clasping, **rough on both sides, strongly veined, sharply toothed,** flowers violet, heads 1 to 1½ inches wide in flat-topped clusters. Frequent at low and medium elevations in open or wet areas. Flowers Aug., Sept.

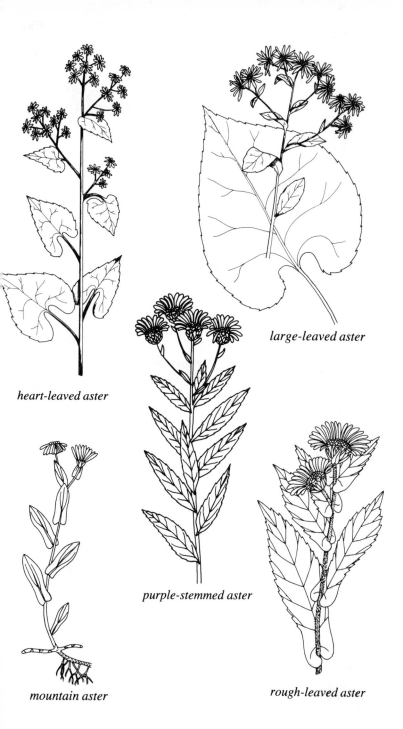

heart-leaved aster

large-leaved aster

purple-stemmed aster

mountain aster

rough-leaved aster

59

BLUE VIOLETS

There are five species of blue violets. All have five-petaled flowers of similar shape but vary in color. They are most easily distinguished by differences in the leaves and habitat.

ALPINE VIOLET   *Viola palustris*

Leaves nearly round, **flowers lilac or nearly white.** Frequent in moist areas and near brooks in the ravines and alpine areas of Washington and Katahdin; also found in the mountains of eastern Canada. Flowers June to Aug.

DOG VIOLET   *Viola adunca*

Plant with a **pair of leaves partway up the stem** (others have leaves only at the base), flowers deep blue. Occasional in moist places on cliffs, and in alpine ravines and alpine areas. Flowers June, July. A very similar species is common in lowland areas.

GREAT-SPURRED VIOLET   *Viola Selkirkii*

Rounded bases of leaves **close together and sometimes overlapping,** flowers pale violet with a **spur on back ¼ inch long.** Occasional in rich woods at low elevations. Flowers in May, earlier than other blue violets. It often grows at the base of a sugar maple.

NORTHERN BLUE VIOLET   *Viola septentrionalis*

Plant 4 to 6 inches high, **leaves heart-shaped, young leaves and stems hairy,** flowers blue. Common in open woods at low elevations. Flowers in May.

MARSH BLUE VIOLET   *Viola cucullata*

Similar to the preceding but **leaves and stem not hairy.** Common in wet places at low elevations. Flowers May, June. A blue violet in a place where there are a lot of mosquitoes is likely to be this one.

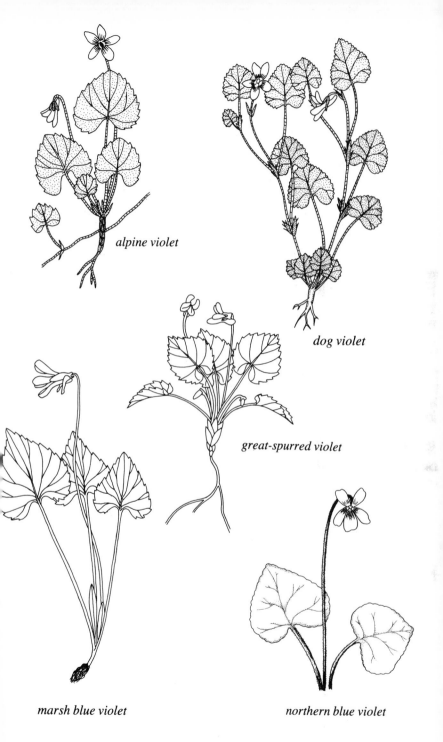

alpine violet

dog violet

great-spurred violet

marsh blue violet

northern blue violet

61

ALPINE SPEEDWELL   *Veronica alpina*

Low, 4 to 8 inches high, **leaves opposite with some teeth,** flowers blue with **4 petals, in a loose spike at the top of the stem.** Occasional near brooks or in ravines and alpine areas of Washington and Katahdin, also in the mountains of eastern Quebec. Flowers July, Aug.

MARSH SKULLCAP   *Scutellaria epilobiifolia*

Plant 1 to 2 feet high, **leaves opposite, stem square,** flowers blue, **2-lipped,** up to 1 inch long, frequent in moist places at low elevations. Flowers July, Aug.

MAD-DOG SKULLCAP   *Scutellaria lateriflora*

Similar to the preceding but **flowers smaller, less than ½ inch long.** Occurs in similar habitats. These two plants are in the mint family, and have the characteristic square stems.

BLUETS   *Houstonia caerulea*

Plant about 3 inches high, leaves small, **opposite,** flowers with 4 petals, **pale blue with a yellow eye in the center,** less than ½ inch across. Occasional in open areas at low elevations. Flowers May, June. This plant may get into the alpine area but the alpine bluet is much more common there.

WHITE LETTUCE   *Lactuca biennis*

Plant 5 feet or more tall, leaves **deeply lobed and coarsely toothed, with a milky juice,** blue flowers in **many small heads ¼ inch across.** Frequent in thickets and open areas. Flowers July to Sept. The flowers of a very similar species are yellow. Although, related to garden lettuce, the leaves are tough and would not make a good salad.

MILK VETCH   *Astragalus Blakeii*

Plant up to 2 feet high, leaves **compound with 5 to 13 leaflets,** flowers blue, **less than ½ inch long,** fruit resembling a small bean pod. Occasional on cliffs at low elevations in Vermont. Flowers May, June; fruits July, Aug.

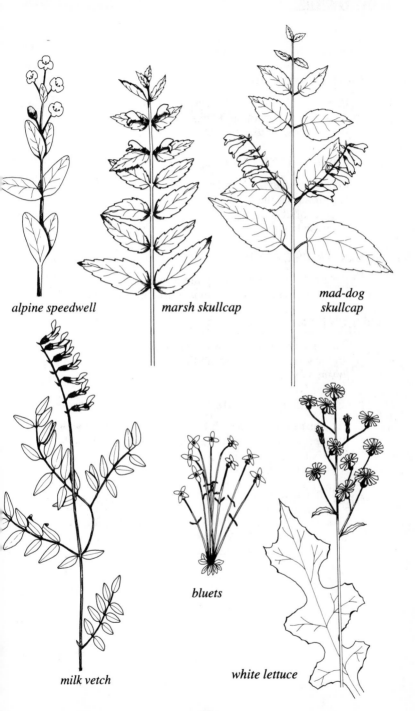

alpine speedwell

marsh skullcap

mad-dog skullcap

milk vetch

bluets

white lettuce

63

Flowers Green or Brown

BRACTED ORCHID   *Habenaria viridis*

Plant 1 to 3 feet tall, flowers green in loose spikes, each **with a long narrow leaf (bract) at its base.** Rare in rich hardwoods on lower slopes. Flowers June to Aug.

ROUND-LEAVED ORCHID   *Habenaria orbiculata*

Plant 1 to 3 feet tall with **2 large shiny nearly round leaves** flat on the ground at the base of the stem, 1 or 2 small leaves near the middle of the stem, flowers pale green 1 inch long. Rare in hardwoods at low elevations. Flowers July, Aug.

HOOKER'S ORCHID   *Habenaria Hookeri*

Resembles round-leaved orchid with 2 leaves at the base but **no leaves on stem.** Occurs in similar habitats. Not illustrated.

BLUNT-LEAVED ORCHID   *Habenaria obtusata*

Plant 6 to 18 inches high with **1 shiny leaf at the base**, spike with a few scattered greenish-white flowers. Rare in evergreen woods at low and medium elevations. Flowers July to Sept.

GREEN WOOD ORCHID   *Habenaria clavellata*

Plant up to 1 foot high with **1 well-developed leaf near the base of the stem and 1 or several much smaller ones above it**, flowers greenish-white in a short spike **1 to 2 inches long.** Occasional in bogs and wet places at low elevations. Flowers July, Aug.

HELLEBORINE ORCHID   *Epipactis helleborine*

Plant about 1 foot high, **stem with several clasping leaves**, flowers greenish-purple. Occasional in open areas at low elevations. Flowers July to Sept. This is a European orchid which has become so well established that in many places it appears to be native.

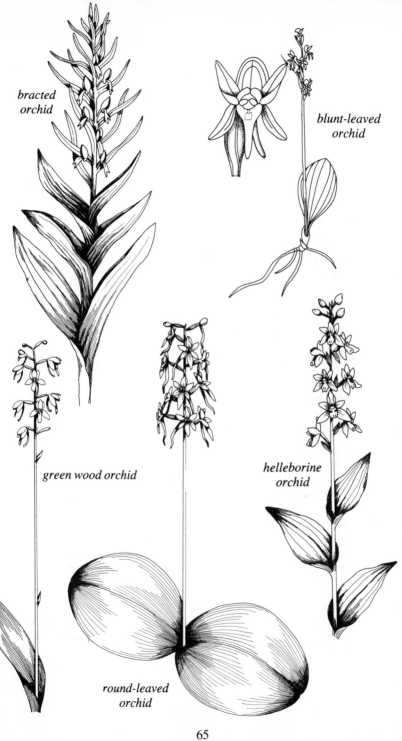

bracted orchid

blunt-leaved orchid

green wood orchid

helleborine orchid

round-leaved orchid

65

JACK-IN-THE-PULPIT   *Arisaema triphyllum*

Plant 1 to 3 feet high, 1 compound leaf with 3 leaflets, **a striped green and purple hood arching over a stalk.** The "jack" has small flowers at its base which are not visible, fruit a cluster of scarlet berries. Common in hardwoods at low elevations. Flowers May, June; fruits July, Aug. If the root is eaten raw it causes a painful stinging sensation which lasts for an hour or more. The Indians had a method of preparing the starchy root so that it could be used for food.

INDIAN POKE   *Veratrum viride*

Plant up to 5 feet high with a stout stem, **leaves large, oval, strongly ribbed lengthwise and clasping the stem,** greenish-yellow flowers often do not develop. Common in moist woods at low elevations, frequent in alpine ravines and moist alpine meadows. Flowers June, July. The large leaves are conspicuous in early spring and are often mistaken for skunk cabbage. The root and leaves are poisonous.

SOLOMON'S SEAL   *Polygonatum biflorum*

This plant has greenish-yellow flowers and is described in the yellow section.

MOUNTAIN TWISTED STALK   *Streptopus amplexifolius*

Resembles purple twisted stalk in aspect. Plant up to 3 feet high, **forked stem and pale green clasping leaves,** flowers greenish with 6 parts, bell-shaped, fruit a red berry. Frequent in hardwoods at low elevations, also in alpine ravines and moist alpine meadows. Flowers late May in the lowlands; June, July in the alpine zone. In the alpine area it intergrades with purple twisted stalk, making identification difficult.

BROAD-LEAVED TWAYBLADE   *Listera convallarioides*

Plant up to 1 foot high, **nearly round leaves near the middle of the stem,** slightly hairy on the upper part, flowers greenish-white. Rare in damp or mossy woods at low elevations. Flowers June to Aug. This wildflower is inconspicuous and only sharp eyes will find it.

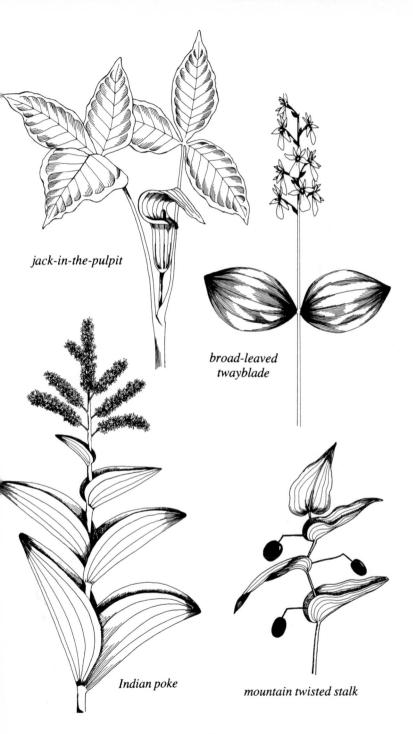

jack-in-the-pulpit

broad-leaved twayblade

Indian poke

mountain twisted stalk

NORTHERN TOADFLAX   *Geocaulon lividum*

Plant up to 1 foot tall, stem with **alternate leaves about 1 inch long**, flowers greenish, inconspicuous, fruit a scarlet berry. Rare in damp woods on mountain slopes to high elevations but not in the alpine area. Flowers June, July. When not in flower it looks much like a low blueberry plant.

MOUNTAIN SORREL   *Oxyria digyna*

Low plant about 8 inches high, **leaves mostly at the base, nearly round,** stem rather stout, flowers greenish-brown in a compact cluster. Occasional in wet places in ravines and in the alpine area on Washington, widespread in the Arctic. Flowers June, July. This plant is related to the garden sorrel whose flowers and seed pods are similar.

MEADOW RUE   *Thalictrum polygamum*

The flowers may have a greenish aspect, but this plant is described in the white section.

BLUE COHOSH   *Caulophyllum thalictroides*

Plant 1 to 3 feet high, **1 large compound leaf in the middle of the stem**, leaflets bluish-green, flowers greenish-yellow or purplish with 6 parts, about ½ inch wide, fruit a blue berry. Occasional in rich woods at low elevations. Flowers May to mid-June; fruits July, Aug.

GOLDEN SAXIFRAGE   *Chrysosplenium americanum*

Low matted plant, leaves nearly round under ½ inch long, flowers tiny, greenish-yellow. Frequent in wet places at low and medium elevations. Another name for the plant is "water carpet," as it frequently covers mud with its green leaves.

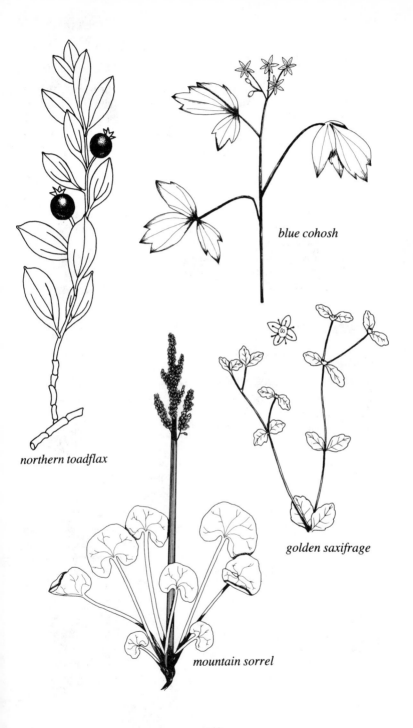

blue cohosh

northern toadflax

golden saxifrage

mountain sorrel

BEECHDROPS   *Epifagus virginiana*

Plant 6 to 18 inches high, **stem with no green leaves**, flowers small, scattered along the stem, whitish with purple-brown splotches. Common in beech woods at low elevations. Flowers Aug. to Oct. This plant is a parasite on the roots of beech trees, though it does the trees no appreciable harm.

EYEBRIGHT   *Euphrasia Williamsii*

Low plant, 1 to 3 inches high, **leaves opposite with round teeth** up to ½ inch long, **flowers very small, brownish or maroon.** Rare in the alpine zones of Washington and Katahdin, also in the mountains of eastern Canada. Flowers July, Aug. A very similar plant with whitish flowers was formerly considered a separate species but now is considered a color-variant of this one. The name "eye-bright" presumably refers to the fact that it takes sharp eyes to find it.

WATER STARWORT   *Callitriche palustris*

Aquatic, usually growing in water but occasionally stranded in mud, leaves narrow up to ½ inch long, flowers very small with stamens and pistils but not petals, fruit a small seed at the base of the leaf. Occasional in pools and ponds at low and medium elevations. Flowers in June; fruits July, Aug.

SNOWBERRY   *Gaultheria hispidula*

This prostrate plant with a slightly woody stem, very small flowers, and white berries is described in the shrub section.

RATTLESNAKE ROOT   *Prenanthes trifoliata*

Plant 1 to 3 feet high, leaves variable in shape but usually **lobed or divided into 3 parts**, flowers greenish-white. Frequent in open areas at low elevations, and in the alpine zone, where it is usually much shorter. Flowers Aug., Sept.

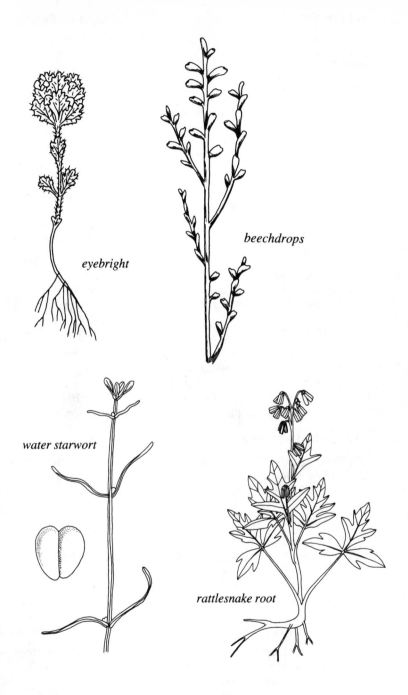

eyebright

beechdrops

water starwort

rattlesnake root

Flowers Red or Orange

WOOD LILY   *Lilium philadelphicum*

Plant up to 3 feet high, **leaves in whorls**, 1 to 5 orange flowers with purple spots. Fruit a pod 1 inch or more long. Occasional on or near dry ledges at low elevations. Flowers mid-June to mid-July.

CANADA LILY   *Lilium canadense*

This plant sometimes has orange flowers but usually yellow ones. It is described in the yellow section.

RED TRILLIUM   *Trillium erectum*

Stem about 1 foot high, **a whorl of 3 leaves at the top**, 1 flower deep red with 3 petals and an unpleasant odor. Common in hardwoods at low and medium elevations. Flowers late April to May. The malodorous flower attracts insects which aid in pollination.

WILD GINGER   *Asarum canadense*

Low plant with **2 large heart-shaped leaves at the base**, flowers purple-brown with 3 petals at the base of the leaf and partly hidden by the leaves. Occasional at low elevations in Maine and Vermont, rare in New Hampshire. Flowers late April to May. The root tastes like ginger, but the plant is not related to the commercial variety.

WILD COLUMBINE   *Aquilegia canadensis*

Plant up to 3 feet high, leaves compound, **flowers scarlet with a yellow center**, petals with a spur at the back. Frequent on ledges and cliffs at low elevations. Flowers in May.

PITCHER PLANT   *Sarracenia purpurea*

Leaves pitcher-shaped and hollow, usually half-filled with water, stem of flower about 1 foot high with a nodding dark red flower at the top. Frequent in acid bogs at low elevations. Flowers June to Aug. Stiff, downward pointing hairs on the leaves trap insects, which are then digested by plant juices and fertilize the plant.

MARSH ST. JOHNSWORT   *Hypericum virginicum*

Plant 1 to 2 feet high, **leaves opposite and with a reddish tinge**, flowers with 5 petals, red to pink. Frequent in wet places and bogs at low elevations. Flowers July, Aug.

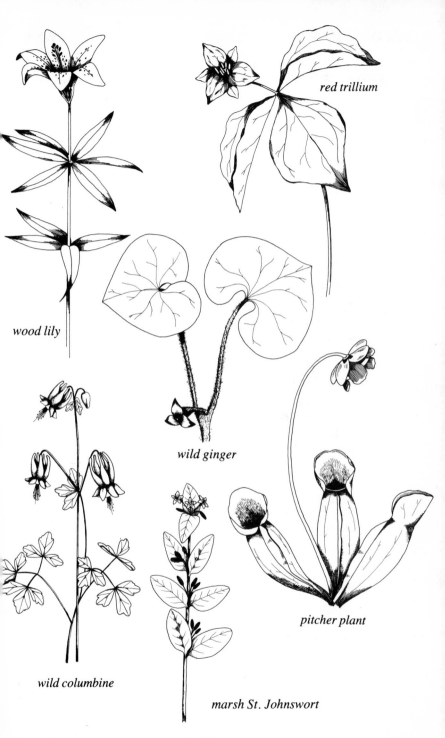

red trillium

wood lily

wild ginger

wild columbine

marsh St. Johnswort

pitcher plant

Flowers White   *Irregular*

WHITE FRINGED ORCHID   *Habenaria belphariglottis*

Plant 1 to 2 feet high, stem with several leaves, **flowers pure white, front petal (lip) with conspicuous fringes.** Rare in bogs at low elevations. Flowers mid-July to mid-Aug.

WHITE ORCHID   *Habenaria dilatata*

Plant 1 to 3 feet high, stem leafy, flowers white **in a long slender spike, front petal not fringed.** Frequent in wet areas at low and medium elevations and in alpine ravines. Flowers mid-June to Aug.

RATTLESNAKE PLANTAIN   *Goodyera tesselata*

Plant 6 to 12 inches high, leaves basal, **1 to 2 inches long, criss-crossed with a network of pale lines,** flowers in a **loose spiral.** Occasional in coniferous woods at low and medium elevations. Flowers July, Aug.

DWARF RATTLESNAKE PLANTAIN   *Goodyera repens*

Smaller than the preceding, plant 4 to 8 inches high, **leaves up to 1 inch long, green, veined with white,** flowers white in a one-sided spike. Occasional in coniferous woods at low and medium elevations. Flowers July, Aug.

LADIES' TRESSES   *Spiranthes cernua*

Plant about 1 foot high, **narrow leaves mostly at the base,** flowers white in a spike. Occasional in wet places in open areas at low elevations. Flowers mid-Aug. to Sept.

DUTCHMAN'S BREECHES   *Dicentra cucullaria*

Delicate plant with a **compound, finely divided, bluish-green leaf,** flowers white-tipped and the white is cream colored or white, tipped with cream color; spurs at top of flower widely spreading and pointed. Occasional in rich hardwoods at low elevations. Flowers late April, May. The flower shape suggests a pair of breeches hanging up to dry.

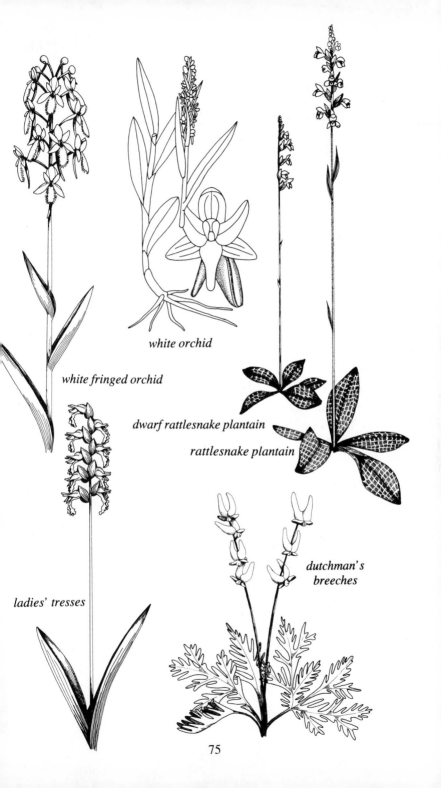

white orchid

white fringed orchid

dwarf rattlesnake plantain

rattlesnake plantain

dutchman's
breeches

ladies' tresses

75

SQUIRREL CORN *Dicentra canadensis*

Similar to the preceding but **spurs at the top of the flower short and rounded,** flowers white or greenish-white. Occasional in rich woods at low elevations. Flowers late April, May. The tubers on the root resemble peas or kernels of corn.

WHITE VIOLET *Viola pallens*

Leaves all basal, heart-shaped, about **1 inch long and about as wide**, flowers white with purple veins. Common at low and medium elevations, often in wet places. Flowers May, June.

KIDNEY-LEAVED VIOLET *Viola renifolia*

Similar to the preceding, leaves heart-shaped and **broader than long**, flowers white with purple stripes. Occasional in hardwoods at low elevations. Flowers mid-April, May. This plant blooms earlier than the white violet. The Latin term, *renifolia,* means kidney-leaved.

BUGLEWEED *Lycopus uniflorus*
or WATER HOREHOUND

Stem square up to 1 foot high, **leaves opposite, coarsely toothed**, with small white flowers at the base. Frequent in wet places at low elevations. Flowers July to Sept.

WATER HOREHOUND *Lycopus americanus*

Similar to the preceding but lower leaves **deeply lobed at the base.** Occurs in similar habitats. Leaf illustrated with bugleweed.

TURTLEHEAD *Chelone glabra*

Plant 1 to 3 feet high, **leaves opposite, toothed**, flowers 1 inch long, white and sometimes tinged with pink. Frequent in swamps and wet places at low elevations. Flowers July to Sept. The shape of the flower resembles a turtle's head.

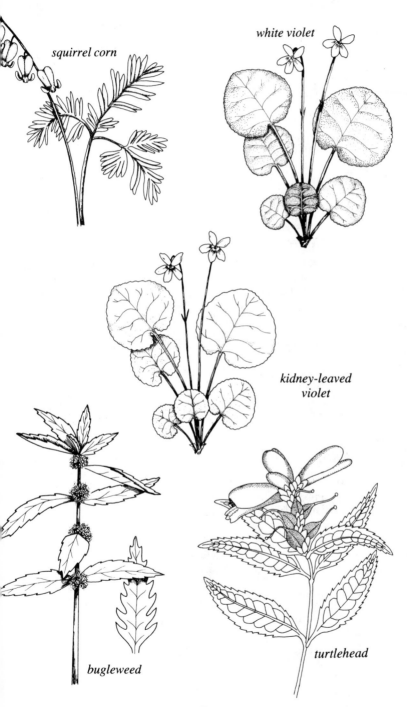

squirrel corn

white violet

kidney-leaved violet

bugleweed

turtlehead

COWWHEAT
Melampyrum lineare

Plant 6 to 18 inches high, **leaves opposite, narrow, about 1 inch long,** flowers whitish with a **yellow tip**, less than ½ inch long. Occasional in dry woods and open areas at low and medium elevations, sometimes higher. Flowers July, Aug.

EYEBRIGHT
Euphrasia Williamsii

One form of this very small alpine plant has white flowers. It is described in the brown section.

Flowers White
2, 3, or 4 petals

ENCHANTER'S NIGHTSHADE
Circaea alpina

Low plant less than 1 foot high, **leaves toothed, opposite,** flowers white in a loose spike with **very small petals**, about ⅛ inch long, fruit a small clinging burr. Common in moist areas and in swamps at low elevations. Flowers mid-June to Aug. The plant was named by the ancient Greeks for Circe, the enchantress.

PAINTED TRILLIUM
Trillium undulatum

Stem about 1 foot high, **a whorl of 3 leaves at the top,** 1 flower with 3 white petals with red or purple stripes at the base. Common in hardwoods at low elevations. Flowers May, June. This plant resembles red trillium but the color of the flower is significantly different.

CANADA MAYFLOWER
Maianthemum canadense

Small plant up to 6 inches high, **2 or 3 heart-shaped leaves,** flowers white with 4 petals, fruit a speckled red berry. Common in woodlands from low to high elevations, frequent in grassy places in the alpine zone. Flowers May, June; fruits July, Aug.

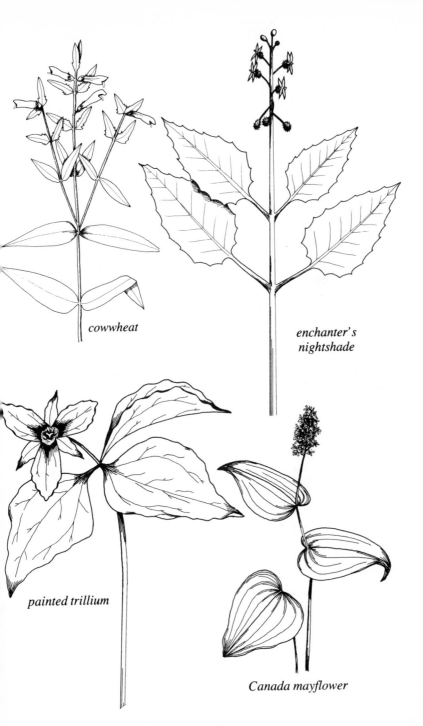

cowwheat

enchanter's
nightshade

painted trillium

Canada mayflower

WILDFLOWERS

White

BEDSTRAWS

The bedstraws have square stems, leaves in whorls of 4 to 8, and tiny white flowers. The species likely to be found in the mountains are described here.

SWEET-SCENTED BEDSTRAW   *Galium triflorum*

Plant 1 to 2 feet high with a weak stem, **leaves in whorls of 6's,** flowers greenish-white, fruit small, round and densely bristled. Frequent in woods at low and medium elevations. Flowers June to Sept. The dried plants are often sweet-scented.

NORTHERN BEDSTRAW   *Galium kamtschaticum*

Plant up to 1 foot high, stem weak, **leaves more than half as broad as long,** in whorls of 4's, flowers yellowish-white, fruit finely bristled. Occasional in woods at low and medium elevations. Flowers June to Aug.

MARSH BEDSTRAW   *Galium palustre*

Plant up to 2 feet high, stem weak, **leaves very narrow, about ½ inch long,** in whorls of 4 or occasionally more, flowers white and sometimes rose-tinged on **horizontally divergent stalks,** fruits smooth. Frequent in wet places at low and medium elevations. Flowers June to Aug.

SMALL BEDSTRAW   *Galium trifidum*

Similar to the preceding but **flower stalks nearly erect.** Occurs in similar habitats.

ALPINE BLUET   *Houstonia caerulea var. Faxonorum*

Plant about 3 inches high, leaves small, opposite, flowers with 4 petals, **white with a yellow eye in the center,** less than ½ inch across. Frequent in alpine ravines and the alpine area of Washington. Flowers June to Sept. This plant is not considered a different species but rather a variety of the lowland bluet (page 62). While the two plants seem distinct to most observers, they are most easily differentiated by elevation. Not illustrated.

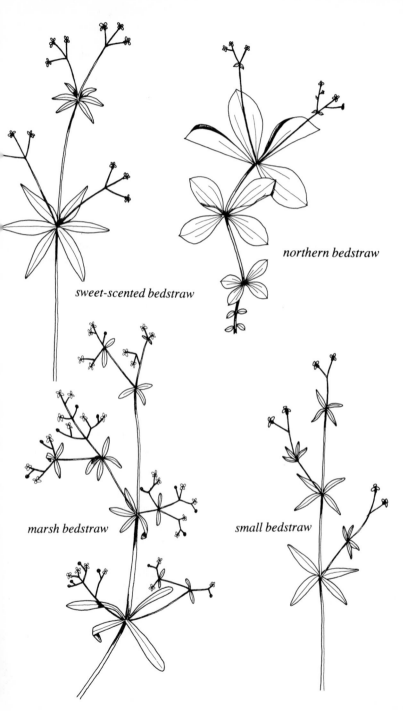

sweet-scented bedstraw

northern bedstraw

marsh bedstraw

small bedstraw

81

ALPINE CRESS   *Cardamine bellidifolia*

Dwarf tufted plant up to 3 inches high, leaves mostly basal on slender stalks up to ¼ inch long, flowers small, white with **4 petals**, fruit a narrow pod about 1 inch long. Occasional near brooks or on wet rocks in alpine ravines and the alpine zone on Katahdin, Washington, and Lafayette, also in the mountains of eastern Canada. Flowers June to Aug.; fruits July to Sept.

BITTER CRESS   *Cardamine pensylvanica*

Plant 6 to 18 inches high, basal leaves nearly round, **stem leaves compound with a number of leaflets,** flowers white, **small up to ¼ inch wide with 4 petals**, fruit a narrow pod up to 1 inch long. Frequent in wet places and in brooks at low elevations and occasionally higher. Flowers May to Aug. The leaves have a pleasant pungent flavor and are a good substitute for watercress.

ROCK CRESS   *Arabis Drummondi*

Plant 1 to 3 feet high, **stem with numerous narrow leaves,** flowers white or pale purple with **4 petals**, fruit a pod up to 3 inches long. Occasional on ledges at low elevations, also in alpine ravines. Flowers in May in the lowlands, June, July in the alpine area.

BUNCHBERRY   *Cornus canadensis*

Stem 3 to 6 inches high with a **single whorl of 6 leaves**, occasionally more or less, flowers with **4 large white petallike parts** surrounding a number of small greenish flowers in the center, fruit a cluster of red berries. Common in woods at all elevations, frequent near krummholz in the alpine zone. Flowers May, June in the lowlands and June, July at high elevations; fruits July to Sept. The berries are not poisonous but have an insipid flavor.

PARTRIDGEBERRY   *Mitchella repens*

Trailing plant with opposite leaves, ½ to 1 inch long, **often with white veins,** flowers white with 4 petals, fruit a scarlet berry. Common in woods at low elevations. Flowers June, July; fruits July to Nov. The berries are said to be edible although partridges eat them more often than humans. The leaves remain green until late in the year and the plant is sometimes used for Christmas wreaths.

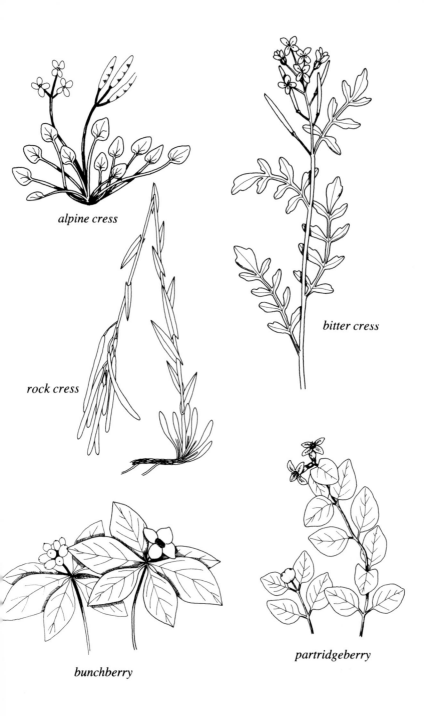

alpine cress

bitter cress

rock cress

bunchberry

partridgeberry

83

Flowers White   *5 Petals, Leaves Opposite*

WHITLOWWORT   *Paronychia argyrocoma*

Low tufted plant up to 5 inches high, **leaves narrow about ¼ inch long,** flowers resembling a **mass of whitish-gray, chaffy scales.** Occasional on dry cliffs or rocky summits at low and medium elevations. Flowers June to Sept. The flowers are nondescript but the plant is distinctive.

GREENLAND   *Arenaria groenlandica*
or MOUNTAIN SANDWORT

Low tufted plant up to 6 inches high, often forming mats, **leaves opposite, narrow, about ¼ inch long,** flowers white about ½ inch wide. Common on ledges and bare summits at medium elevations and in the alpine zone. Flowers June to Aug. As the name suggests, this plant is also found in Greenland. It is one of the few alpine plants to remain in bloom throughout the summer season.

REDDISH SANDWORT   *Arenaria rubella*

Resembles Greenland sandwort but with many **narrow crowded leaves with 3 prominent ribs** at the base of the stem. Rare on cliffs at low elevations in Vermont. Flowers June to Aug.

NORTHERN SANDWORT   *Arenaria marcescens*

Low tufted plant with a partly woody stem, **many narrow crowded leaves,** leaves wither quickly but remain attached to stem. Rare in Vermont and in Quebec. Flowers July, Aug.

MOUNTAIN STITCHWORT   *Stellaria calycantha*

Weak reclining plant up to 1 foot high with **narrow, opposite leaves up to ½ inch long,** flowers small, white, less than ¼ inch across. Occasional near brooks at low elevations, more common in the alpine zone. Flowers June to Sept.

MITERWORT   *Mitella diphylla*

Stem 6 to 18 inches high with **pair of opposite leaves about halfway up,** flowers small, white, **each petal fringed.** Occasional in hardwoods at low elevations. Flowers May, June.

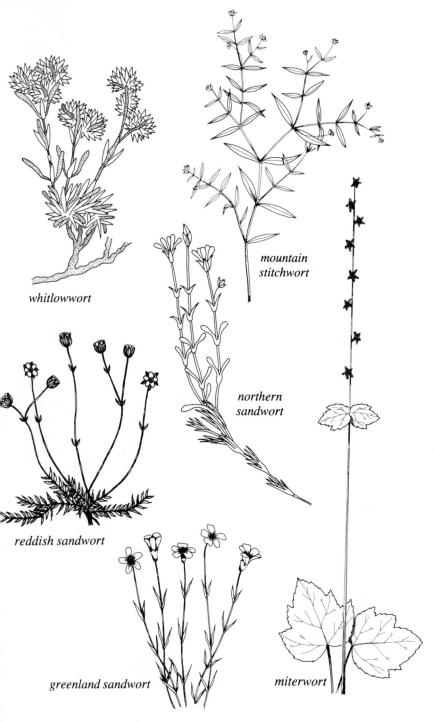

whitlowwort

*mountain
stitchwort*

*northern
sandwort*

reddish sandwort

greenland sandwort

miterwort

85

DIAPENSIA
Diapensia lapponica

Low tufted plant forming dense cushions, leaves up to ½ inch long, crowded, flowers white. Common in alpine areas, also in the Arctic. Flowers late May, June. The "cushions" of the plant presumably help to retain heat.

Flowers White
5 Petals, Leaves Basal

GOLDTHREAD
Coptis groenlandica

Leaves compound, divided into 3 leaflets, **shiny and evergreen,** stalk 2 to 6 inches high with a single flower at the top, white with 5 petallike parts. Common in woods at all elevations and in alpine zone. Flowers May, July. The bright yellow root tastes bitter.

DALIBARBA or DEWDROP
Dalibarba repens

Plant 3 inches high, **leaves heart-shaped with a scalloped margin,** flowers ½ inch wide with numerous stamens. Frequent in woods at low elevations. Flowers July, Aug.

SUNDEW
Drosera rotundifolia

Plant up to 3 inches high, leaves small, about ½ inch long on **long stalks covered with knob-tipped sticky hairs,** flowers small in a one-sided curving spike. Frequent in bogs and wet places at low and medium elevations. Flowers June to Aug. The hairs trap and coil around insects, which are then broken down into soil nutrients.

EARLY SAXIFRAGE
Saxifraga virginiensis

Plant 4 to 12 inches high, **leaves egg-shaped, toothed,** ½ to 3 inches long, flowers in branching clusters. Common on ledges and in rocks at low elevations. Flowers in May. The Latin name, *saxifraga*, means rock-breaking, referring to the belief that the plant's juices when ingested would break up kidney stones.

MOUNTAIN BROOK SAXIFRAGE
Saxifraga rivularis

Low tufted plant about 3 inches high, **leaves divided into 3 to 7 lobes,** thin flowering stalks bearing 1 to 5 flowers. Rare in wet areas on Washington, widespread in the Arctic. Flowers July, Aug. This plant has appeared spontaneously near the Tip Top House and Lakes of the Clouds hut on Washington.

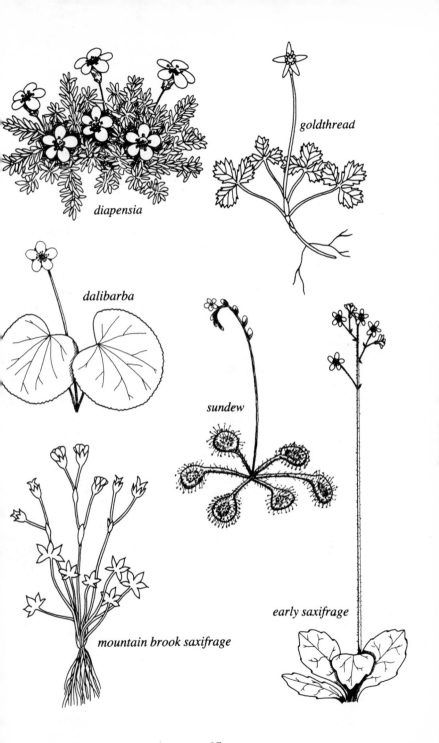

diapensia

goldthread

dalibarba

sundew

mountain brook saxifrage

early saxifrage

87

LIME-LEAVED SAXIFRAGE
Saxifraga aizoon

Plant 4 to 6 inches high, **leaves covered with conspicuous lime-encrusted pores,** a cluster of flowers at the top of the stem. Rare on rocks in the alpine regions of Washington and Katahdin, and on cliffs at low elevations in Vermont. There is only one small colony on Washington, but as it can be reached only by rock climbers it is probably in no danger of extermination.

STAR SAXIFRAGE
Saxifraga stellaris

Low plant up to 6 inches high, **leaves all basal, narrow, widening at the end with some teeth,** flowers mostly replaced by **leafy tufts,** but in large plants a single white flower at the top. Rare on Katahdin, more common in the Arctic. Flowers July, Aug. This plant may have been fairly common on Katahdin at one time; it has now been nearly exterminated from over-collecting by botanists and trampling by hikers.

FOAMFLOWER
Tiarella cordifolia

Plant 6 to 12 inches high, leaves on slender stalks, **shaped like a maple leaf,** white flowers in a loose spike with conspicuous stamens that produce the foamy appearance. Frequent in woods at low elevations. Flowers May, June.

NAKED MITERWORT
Mitella nuda

Plant up to 8 inches high, **leaves roundly heart-shaped with scalloped teeth,** flowers small in a thin spike. Occasional in hardwoods at low and medium elevations. Flowers May to July.

STRAWBERRY
Fragaria virginiana

Plant 3 to 12 inches high, **leaves compound with 3 sharply toothed leaflets,** flowers white in a flat-topped cluster with stamens and pistils prominent. Fruit a red berry with small seeds deeply imbedded in its surface. Common in open places at low elevations, occasional in alpine ravines. Flowers May, June; fruits June, July. The berries are small and picking them is laborious, but they have a fine flavor and many people consider them the tastiest of the wild fruits.

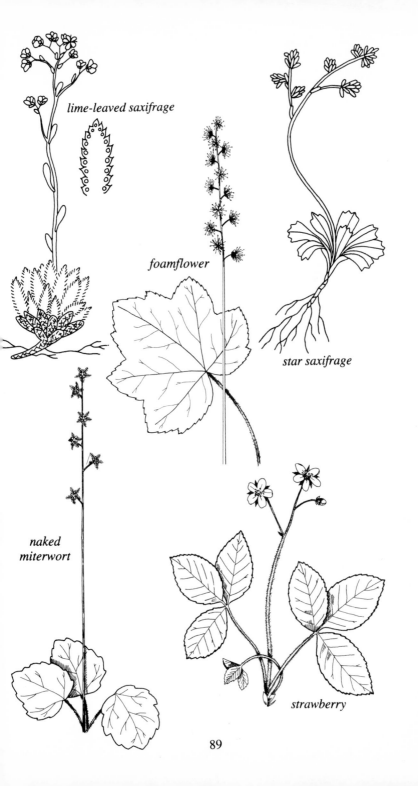

lime-leaved saxifrage

foamflower

star saxifrage

naked miterwort

strawberry

89

MOUNTAIN STRAWBERRY   *Fragaria vesca*

Similar to the preceding but **flowers on stalks of varying lengths,** fruit cone-shaped with the **seeds on the surface.** Occasional in rocky woods or on cliffs at low elevations. Flowers May, June; fruits June, July.

MOUNTAIN WOOD SORREL   *Oxalis montana*

Delicate plant up to 4 inches high, **leaves compound, with 3 leaflets notched at the tips,** flowers white, **veined with pink.** Common in woods at all elevations and under krummholz in the alpine zone. Flowers June to Aug. Mats of leaves, without flowers, are often seen in the woods.

WILD SARSAPARILLA   *Aralia nudicaulis*

Single leaf large and **compound, divided into 3 groups of 5 leaflets,** spreading and parallel to the ground, about 1 foot high, flowers small, greenish-white in a ball-shaped cluster, fruit a purplish-black berry. Common in woods at low elevations. Flowers June, July. The root has a pleasant aromatic flavor and was formerly used as an ingredient in a drink called sarsaparilla.

ONE-SIDED PYROLA   *Pyrola secunda*

Stem 3 to 8 inches tall, leaves evergreen, flowers white or greenish-white **on one side of the flowering stem,** pistil protruding from flower. Frequent in woods in dry and moist places at low elevations. Flowers July, Aug.

PYROLA   *Pyrola elliptica*
or SHINLEAF

Stem 4 to 12 inches high, leaves 1 to 3 inches long, evergreen, flowers white with **spreading petals and prominent pistil.** Frequent at low elevations. Flowers July, Aug.

LESSER PYROLA   *Pyrola minor*

Smaller than the preceding, up to 8 inches high, leaves about 1 inch long and nearly round, flowers white or pinkish, **nearly round with the petals almost meeting at the top.** Occasional in evergreen woods at low and medium elevations. Flowers July to mid-Aug.

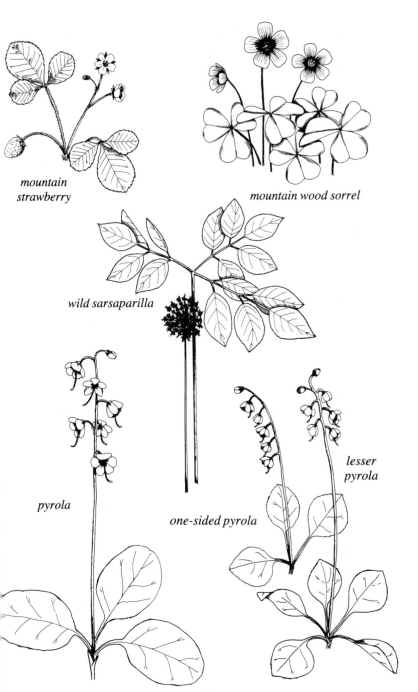

mountain
strawberry

mountain wood sorrel

wild sarsaparilla

pyrola

one-sided pyrola

lesser
pyrola

91

ONE-FLOWERED CANCERROOT   *Orobanche uniflora*

Leaves basal, small and scalelike, stem white about 6 inches with a whitish tubular curved flower at the top. Occasional in woods at low elevations. Flowers May to July. This plant is a parasite, drawing its nourishment from the roots of other plants.

Flowers White   *5 Petals, Leaves Alternate and Simple*

ALPINE BISTORT   *Polygonum viviparum*

Plant 4 to 12 inches high, basal leaves less than ½ inch broad on long stalks, flowers white or pinkish in a **tight thin spike, the lower flowers replaced by bulbets.** Common in alpine areas of Washington and Katahdin, also in the Arctic. Flowers June to Aug.

BINDWEED   *Polygonum cilinode*
or FALSE BUCKWHEAT

Slender, twining vine with a weedy aspect, **leaves heart-shaped,** flowers small white or greenish in loose spikelike clusters, fruit a triangular seed about ⅛ inch long. Frequent on ledges and talus at low elevations. Flowers June to Aug.

NODDING SAXIFRAGE   *Saxifraga cernua*

Stem about 6 inches high with **pale bulbets at the base,** basal leaves heart-shaped, upper leaves narrow, **a single small white flower at the top of the stem.** Rare in alpine regions on Washington, more common in the Arctic. Flowers mid-July to mid-Aug. The one known location of the plant on Washington can only be reached by rock climbers.

CLOUDBERRY   *Rubus Chamaemorus*

Plant 6 to 18 inches high, **leaves with 3 shallow lobes, single white flower ½ to 1 inch wide** at the top of the stem, fruit a reddish or yellowish berry, resembling a raspberry. Rare in bogs at all elevations in mountains of western Maine and northern New Hampshire, widespread in the Arctic. Flowers June, July; fruits July, Aug. The berries are said to be very good, but it is hard to find enough to make a meal.

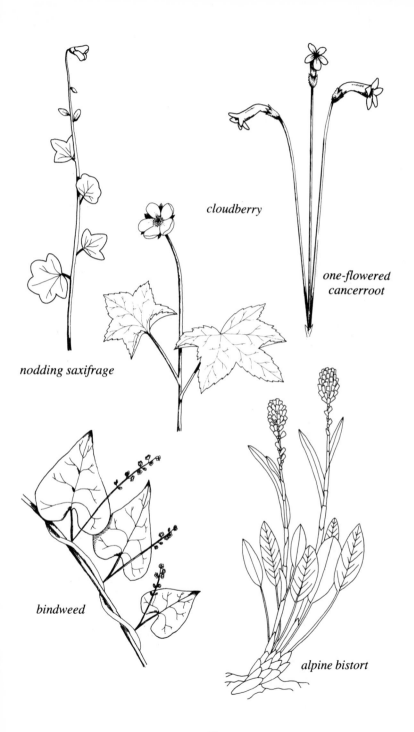

cloudberry

one-flowered
cancerroot

nodding saxifrage

bindweed

alpine bistort

WATER PENNYWORT
Hydrocotyle americana

Low plant up to 3 inches high with a **creeping stem,** leaves round and heart-shaped with scalloped edges, **flowers tiny, less than ¼ inch across.** Frequent in moist areas at low elevations. Flowers June to Sept.

INDIAN PIPE
Monotropa uniflora

Plant about 6 inches high, **stem and scaly leaves white,** a single nodding flower at the top of the stem. Frequent in woods at low and medium elevations. Flowers June to Sept. This plant is a parasite. Having no green leaves, it cannot make food and must receive nourishment from the roots of other plants.

MAYFLOWER or TRAILING ARBUTUS
Epigaea repens

Trailing shrub with a slightly woody stem, **leaves evergreen and leathery, oval, 1 to 3 inches long,** flowers white or pink in small clusters at the tips of the stems. Frequent in woods at low elevations. Flowers mid-April to May.

CHECKERBERRY
Gaultheria procumbens

Stem up to 6 inches high with **several dark green and shiny leaves near the top,** leaves obscurely toothed, flowers white, bell-shaped, ¼ inch long, fruit a bright red berry. Common in woods at low and medium elevations. Flowers July, Aug.; fruits Aug. to Nov. The berries are edible, and the leaves have a pleasant flavor of wintergreen.

PIPSISSEWA
Chimaphilia umbellata

Plant up to 1 foot high, **leaves dark green, shiny, evergreen,** 1 or 2 inches long, **alternate or more often in whorls,** flowers waxy white or pinkish, about ½ inch wide. Frequent in dry woods at low elevations. Flowers July, Aug.

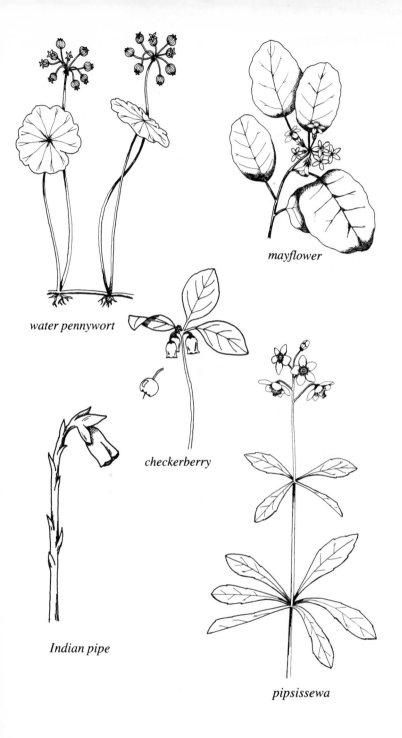

water pennywort

mayflower

checkerberry

Indian pipe

pipsissewa

Flowers White   *5 Petals, Leaves Alternate and Compound*

THREE-TOOTHED CINQUEFOIL   *Potentilla tridentata*

Leaves with 3 leaflets, **3-toothed at the top, evergreen and shiny,** stem up to 1 foot high, with several white flowers at the top up to 1 inch wide in a branched cluster. Common in open gravelly or rocky areas at all elevations and in the alpine zone. Flowers June to Sept.

BLACKBERRY and RASPBERRY

These are described in the shrub section with the exception of the herbaceous dwarf raspberry.

DWARF RASPBERRY   *Rubus pubescens*

Main stem trailing with no prickles, erect flowering stems up to 1 foot high with compound leaves of 3 to 5 leaflets, flowers up to ½ inch wide, fruit resembling a raspberry, dark red and juicy. Common in moist areas at low and medium elevations, occasional in alpine ravines and alpine meadows. Flowers June, July; fruits July to Sept. The fruit is edible but sparse.

BRISTLY SARSAPARILLA   *Aralia hispida*

Plant up to 3 feet high, **lower stem bristly,** leaves compound with varying numbers of sharp-toothed leaflets, flowers small, white, in **ball-shaped clusters,** fruit a dark purple berry. Common in open, dry, or sandy soil at low and medium elevations. Flowers June to Aug.

SWEET CICELY   *Osmorhiza Claytoni*

Stem up to 3 feet high, compound leaves divided into a number of lobed and toothed leaflets, **resembles a fern leaf, flowers white, very small** in several flat-topped clusters, fruit a slender pod. Occasional in rich hardwoods at low elevations. Flowers May, June. The root is described as rank-tasting, while that of a similar species, anise root, is aromatic.

three-toothed cinquefoil

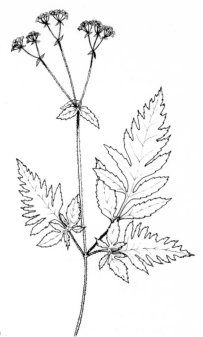

sweet cicely

bristly sarsaparilla

dwarf raspberry

HEMLOCK PARSLEY
Conioselinum chinense

Slender plant up to 5 feet high, compound leaf divided into many leaflets which are in turn divided into **fine narrow segments, resembles one of the more delicate ferns,** flowers small and white in several flat-topped clusters, all arising from the same point at the top of the stem. Occasional on open slopes and cliffs at low and medium elevations. Flowers July to Sept. This plant may be poisonous; it is related to the notorious poison hemlock.

ANGELICA
Angelica atropurpurea

Plant with a **stout purple-stained stem 6 feet or more high,** compound leaf divided into numerous toothed, egg-shaped leaflets, many nearly round clusters of small whitish flowers all arising from the same point at the top of the stem, fruit a large thin papery seed. Occasional along riverbanks at low elevations, also in moist places in alpine ravines. Flowers June, July; fruits July to Sept.

COW PARSNIP
Heracleum maximum

Large plant with stout stem up to 6 feet tall, **leaves large, often 1 foot broad,** divided into cut-toothed leaflets, flowers small, white, **flower clusters 4 to 8 inches broad,** fruit a papery winged seed ¼ inch long. Occasional in moist open areas at low elevations, also in alpine ravines. Flowers June, July; fruits July to Sept.

Flowers White
6 or More Petals

STAR FLOWER
Trientalis borealis

Stem up to 10 inches high with a **whorl of leaves at the top,** 1 or several white flowers with **7 pointed petals** (sometimes more or less) arising from the whorl. Common in woods at all elevations, occasional in the alpine area. Flowers May to Aug.

GOLDTHREAD
Coptis groenlandica

This plant usually has 5 petals but sometimes 6 or 7. It is described in the 5-petals, leaves basal section.

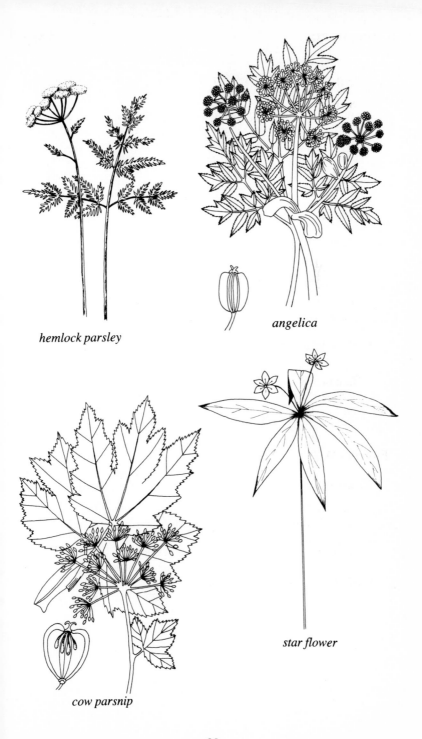

hemlock parsley

angelica

cow parsnip

star flower

FALSE SOLOMON'S SEAL   *Smilacina racemosa*
or FALSE SPIKENARD

Stem 1 to 3 feet tall, **arching and slightly zigzag** with numerous firm leaves on very short stems, flowers small, white with 6 petallike parts in a **large branching cluster at the end of the stem,** fruit a greenish berry, turning red. Common in woods and open areas at low and medium elevations. Flowers mid-May, June; fruits June to Aug.

STAR-FLOWERED SOLOMON'S SEAL   *Smilacina stellata*

Smaller than the preceding, stem 12 to 18 inches tall, erect or only slightly arched, **leaves partly clasping and close together,** flowers white, flower cluster **not branching,** fruit a dark red berry. Occasional at bases of cliffs and along streams at low elevations. Flowers mid-May, June.

THREE-LEAVED SOLOMON'S SEAL   *Smilacina trifolia*

Stem up to 10 inches high with **3 leaves** (sometimes 2 or 4), flower cluster up to 2 inches long, **usually with less than 12 flowers,** fruit a dark red berry. Occasional in bogs and swampy areas at all elevations. Flowers May, June. It somewhat resembles the common Canada mayflower, which has broader leaves, a broader flower cluster, and only 4 petals.

BLOODROOT   *Sanguinaria canadensis*

Stem up to 1 foot high with a **single pale green lobed leaf at the base,** a single white flower with 8 to 12 petals at the top of the stem. Occasional in rich woods at low elevations. Flowers mid-April, May. The juice of the root is orange-red.

BOOTT'S RATTLESNAKE ROOT   *Prenanthes Boottii*

Plant up to 1 foot high, lower leaves triangular or slightly heart-shaped, upper leaves narrow, rather large heads in a spike, each head with **7 or more conspicuous white petallike ray flowers.** Common in the alpine zone. Flowers July to Sept.

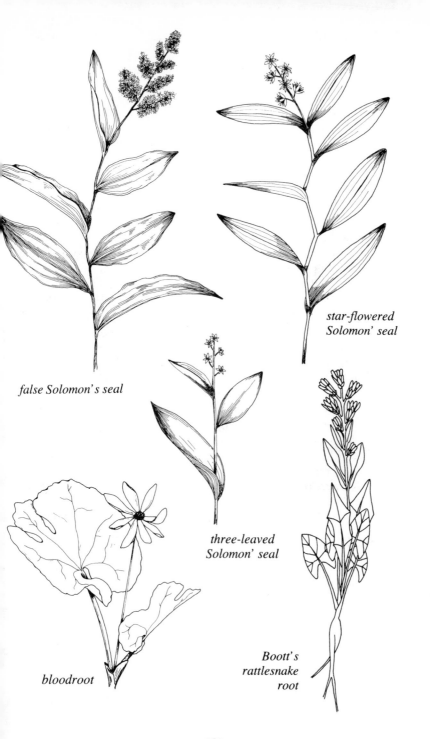

false Solomon's seal

star-flowered Solomon' seal

three-leaved Solomon' seal

bloodroot

Boott's rattlesnake root

FLAT-TOPPED ASTER
Aster umbellatus

Plant 2 to 5 feet tall, leaves numerous, **narrow without teeth,** flowers white with numerous petallike parts (bracts) **in a flat-topped cluster.** Frequent in open moist areas at low elevations, occasional in alpine ravines. Flowers Aug., Sept.

SHARP-LEAVED or WOOD ASTER
Aster acuminatus

Plant 6 inches to 2 feet high, **leaves coarsely toothed and long-pointed, upper leaves appearing as a whorl,** flowers white with numerous narrow drooping petallike parts. Common in woods at low, medium, and occasionally high elevations. Flowers Aug., Sept.

WHITE WOOD ASTER
Aster divaricatus

Plant 1 to 3 feet tall, lower leaves **heart-shaped and coarsely toothed,** flowers white in loose, open, flat-topped clusters. Frequent in woods at low elevations. Flowers Aug, Sept.

Flowers White
Petals or Parts Indistinguishable

PIPEWORT
Eriocaulon septangulare

Leaves basal, narrow and grasslike, stem 1 to 3 feet high bearing at the top a **whitish button-shaped head** consisting of a number of very small flowers surrounded by chaffy scales. Common in shallow water and at edges of ponds at low and medium elevations. Flowers July to Sept.

WHITE BANEBERRY
Actaea pachypoda

Plant 1 to 3 feet high, **leaves compound and divided into many toothed, egg-shaped leaflets,** flowers white on **short thick stalks** with prominent stamens and very small inconspicuous petals, fruit a white berry with a conspicuous purple eye. Frequent in hardwoods at low elevations. Flowers mid-May, June; fruits July to Oct. The conspicuous white fruits are poisonous.

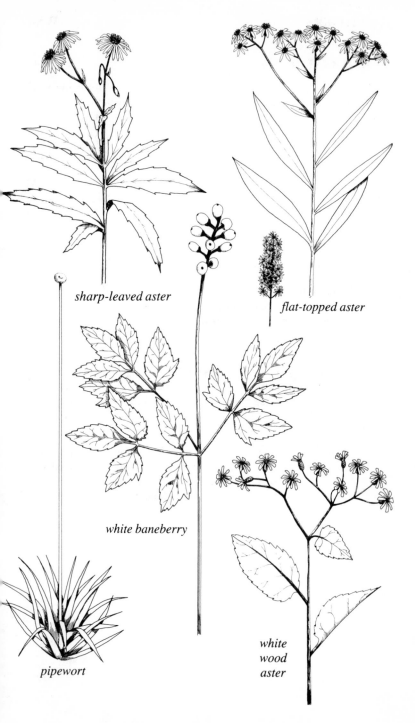

sharp-leaved aster

flat-topped aster

white baneberry

pipewort

white
wood
aster

103

RED BANEBERRY
Actaea rubra

Similar to white baneberry when in flower but **flowering stalks slender, fruit a red berry.** Frequent in hardwoods at low elevations. Flowers mid-May, June. The berries are considered mildly poisonous and have a disagreeable taste.

MEADOW RUE
Thalictrum polygamum

Plant up to 5 feet high, **leaves compound, divided into many separate pale green leaflets,** flowers with 4 small greenish sepals that soon drop, **prominent white, club-shaped stamens.** Common in open areas at low elevations, occasional in alpine ravines. Flowers June to Aug.

WHITE SNAKEROOT
Eupatorium rugosum

Plant up to 3 feet high, **leaves opposite, toothed, flowers bright white** in many heads forming a flat-topped cluster. Occasional in rocky areas at low elevations. Flowers Aug., Sept.

BONESET
Eupatorium perfoliatum

Plant up to 5 feet high, leaves opposite, coarsely toothed, **the bases united around the stem,** flowers in heads as in snakeroot, whitish. Frequent in wet areas at low elevations. Flowers Aug., Sept.

PEARLY EVERLASTING
Anaphalis margaritacea

Plant 1 to 2 feet tall, **stem and underside of leaves white-woolly,** heads composed of numerous **dry white petallike reduced leaves with a yellow tuft in the center.** Frequent in open dry areas, along gravelly banks of streams, and in alpine ravines. Flowers July to Sept.

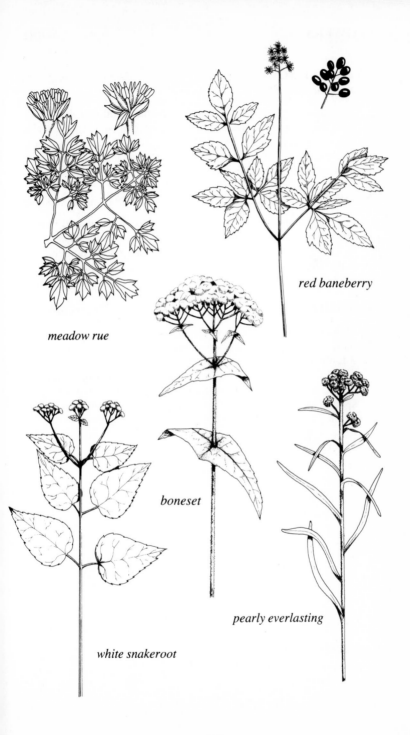

meadow rue

red baneberry

boneset

white snakeroot

pearly everlasting

EVERLASTING or PUSSYTOES
Antennaria neglecta

Stem about 6 inches high, **leafy at the base and forming mats,** stem leaves small, flowers mostly composed of white chaffy scales in a compact cluster. Frequent on ledges at low elevations, occasional on rocky mountaintops. There are similar species which are difficult to differentiate.

MOUNTAIN CUDWEED
Gnaphalium supinum

Low tufted plant up to 4 inches high, **leaves narrow and mostly basal, covered with silky hairs,** 2 to 5 small brownish heads less than ¼ inch high in a crowded spike. Rare on Washington and Katahdin, also on mountains in eastern Canada. Flowers July to Sept.

YARROW
Achillea millefolium

Plant 1 to 3 feet high, **leaves finely divided suggesting a carrot leaf,** heads in a flat-topped cluster, small whitish ray flowers 3-toothed. Occasional in open areas at all elevations. Flowers June to Sept. The lowland plants are weedy and of European origin. In the alpine zone the plant is considered to be native and of a different species, the bracts (small leaflike parts surrounding the heads) having dark margins.

yarrow

everlasting

mountain cudweed

Trees and Shrubs

It is not always easy to distinguish between a small tree and a large shrub. Generally speaking, trees have a single stem and grow to twenty feet or more in height; shrubs are lower and usually have several spreading stems from one base. Some shrubs, however, have a single stem and under favorable conditions grow as tall as trees.

Organization

The trees and shrubs included in this guide range from lowland species to those common on mountain slopes. For easy reference, a list of the latter can be found at the end of this introduction. Trees and shrubs are grouped by families.

Entries

Each entry indicates whether the plant is a tree or shrub (sometimes both) and covers such distinguishing characteristics as size, leaf shape, flowers, fruit and seed cases, habitat (including elevation), and flowering season.

All trees and shrubs have flowers, though those on trees are often inconspicuous. Many shrubs have showy flowers and small shrubs are sometimes considered herbs, or wildflowers. There is a difference, though, between the two: shrubs have woody stems and wildflowers do not. This distinction is not always clear. When in doubt, look for the flowering plant in both the shrub and wildflower sections.

The flowers ripen into fruit, which contains the seeds. Each of these — flowers, fruit, and seed cases — are obvious aids to identification. Perhaps the single most valuable aid in identification, however, is leaf structure. **Opposite leaves** are directly opposite each other on the stem. **Alternate leaves** are on opposite sides of the stem but not at the same level. A **compound leaf** is divided into leaflets attached to a main stem that is not woody.

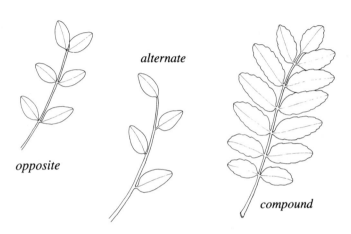

alternate

opposite

compound

Common Trees of Mountain Slopes

DECIDUOUS or
    BROAD-LEAVED

small-tooth aspen or poplar
large-tooth aspen
yellow birch
white birch
heart-leaved white birch
beech
red oak
red cherry
black cherry
sugar maple
red maple
basswood
white ash

EVERGREEN

fir balsam
white spruce
    (Maine and New York)
red spruce
white pine
hemlock
larch
white cedar
    (Maine and New York)
American yew

PINE FAMILY

This family includes trees and a few shrubs and is readily recognized by the needle- or scalelike evergreen leaves. The seeds are usually in cones and these are also a good means of identification. Above 2500 feet the forest is composed mostly of fir balsam and red spruce.

FIR BALSAM   *Abies balsamea*

Tree occasionally up to 60 feet high and 2 feet in diameter but usually smaller. Needles ½ to 1½ inches long **with two white lines on underside,** fragrant when crushed. Cones cylindrical about 1 inch long. Common on mountain slopes at all elevations, a component of the evergreen forest above 2500 feet. In the alpine zone, where it grows in sheltered areas, it is dwarfed and may be matted, forming the alpine krummholz. The fragrant needles and twigs are used for balsam pillows.

WHITE PINE   *Pinus strobus*

Large tree up to 100 feet tall and 3 feet in diameter, **needles 3 to 5 inches long in clusters of 5's.** Occasional on lower slopes and sometimes on bare ledges at medium elevations, where it is much smaller. This is a common lowland tree that does not grow very far up the mountains.

JACK PINE   *Pinus banksiana*

Scrubby tree up to 20 feet high, **needles in clusters of 2's,** shorter than white pine, cones thin and curved. Rare on ledges at low and medium elevations.

HEMLOCK   *Tsuga canadensis*

Tree up to 80 feet high and 3 feet in diameter, needles about ½ inch long with **2 silvery lines beneath,** resembling balsam needles but **irregularly arranged on stem and not fragrant,** cones much smaller than balsam's. Frequent on lower slopes. Twigs bitten off by porcupines are often found under the tree.

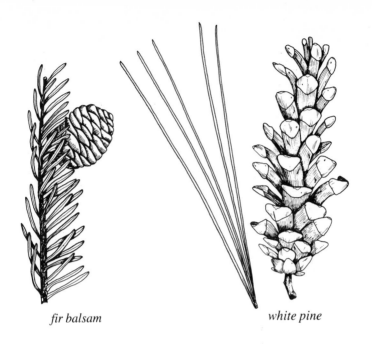

fir balsam

white pine

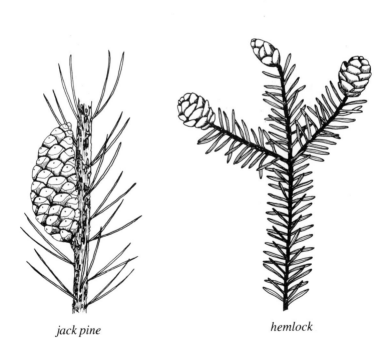

jack pine

hemlock

RED SPRUCE
Picea rubens

Tree up to 80 feet high and 3 feet in diameter. Needles ½ to ¾ inch long, **bright green on top and bottom and somewhat prickly to touch,** cones round or egg-shaped. Common on mountain slopes up to but not in the alpine zone and a component of the evergreen forest above 2500 feet.

BLACK SPRUCE
Picea mariana

Small tree or shrub, needles ½ inch long, **white or bluish-green,** branchlets covered with minute hairs, cones 1 inch long, often remaining on the tree for several years. Occasional on edges of bogs and rocky mountaintops, frequent in alpine areas where it is dwarfed and forms prostrate mats.

WHITE SPRUCE
Picea glauca

Tree up to 60 feet tall, resembles black spruce, needles bluish-green, **twigs pale without any hairs,** crushed needles with a pungent odor. Frequent on mountain slopes in northern Maine and New York. Not illustrated.

LARCH
or TAMARACK
Larix laricina

Tree up to 60 feet tall, needles about 1 inch long in **circular clusters of 10 to 30.** Occasional on mountain slopes in bogs and poorly drained areas, rare in alpine areas as a small bush. Larch is the only pine that loses its needles in winter.

CEDAR FAMILY

WHITE CEDAR
or ARBOR VITAE
Thuja occidentalis

Tree up to 40 feet high, **needles flat and scalelike, closely over-lapping,** crushed needles and twigs aromatic. Frequent at low and medium elevations in northern Maine and the Adirondacks.

JUNIPER
Juniperus communis

Low spreading shrub, **needles thin and sharp with broad white stripe underneath, unpleasant to touch.** Occasional in open areas and on ledges at low elevations, rare in alpine areas where it is a dwarfed. This is a common lowland shrub of old fields.

black spruce

red spruce

larch

white cedar

juniper

113

BEECH FAMILY

BEECH
Fagus grandifolia

Tree up to 60 feet high, leaves 3 to 5 inches long, coarsely toothed with **prominent parallel veins terminating in the teeth, bark hard, smooth, steel-gray,** catkins inconspicuous, producing triangular nuts with edible kernels. Common in the hardwood forest at low elevations. Flowers in May. In a good crop year the nuts provide food for deer and bears. Bear claw scratches can often be seen on beech trees.

RED OAK
Quercus rubra

Tree up to 70 feet high and 3 feet in diameter, **leaves tough and leathery, lobed, with lobes terminating in a bristle,** catkins inconspicuous, producing acorns. Occasional in dry woods at low elevations. Flowers in May. The acorns provide food for birds and other woodland animals. They are bitter but edible if treated to remove the tannin.

LINDEN FAMILY

BASSWOOD
Tilia americana

Large tree up to 100 feet high and 3 feet in diameter, leaves **sharply toothed, unequally heart-shaped at base, often large,** up to 8 inches long. Flowers with yellowish petals, fruit a cluster of nutlets attached to a leafy wing. Occasional in rich hardwoods at low elevations. Flowers in July; fruits in Aug. The dry fruits are sometimes used to make tea.

OLIVE FAMILY

WHITE ASH
Fraxinus americana

Tree up to 80 feet high, leaves and stems **opposite,** leaves **compound with 5 to 7 leaflets,** each up to 4 inches long, flowers small, dark-colored in clusters, fruit a key resembling maple's. Flowers in May; fruits in June.

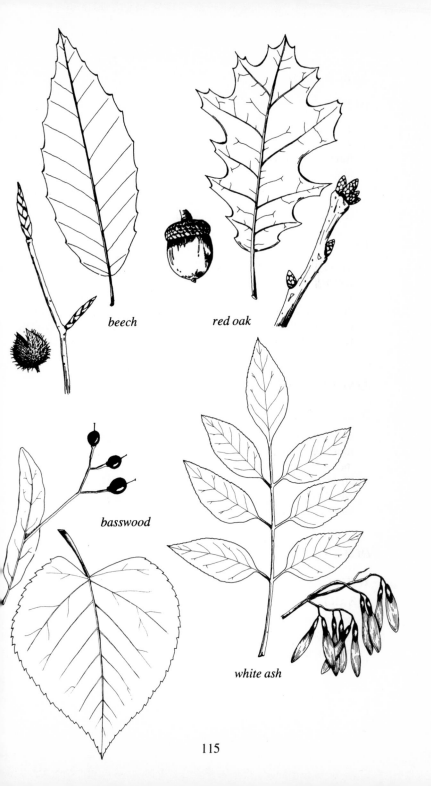

beech

red oak

basswood

white ash

115

BIRCH FAMILY

Trees and shrubs. The brownish drooping catkins that appear in the spring help to identify birches in the alpine zone. At lower elevations the catkins disappear early in the season.

HOPHORNBEAM   *Ostrya virginiana*

Small tree less than 30 feet high, leaves 1 to 4 inches long, sharply toothed, bark gray with **flaky scales which lift up from the edges and cling in the middle.** Occasional in dry woods on the lower slopes.

YELLOW BIRCH   *Betula alleghaniensis*

Tree up to 60 feet high and 3 feet in diameter, leaves heart-shaped at base, double toothed, **bark yellowish or silvery-gray, detaching thin layers.** Common in hardwood forests at low elevations and occuring higher than other hardwoods. Flowers in May. The twigs have a wintergreen flavor. The bark on old trees is close and furrowed.

GRAY BIRCH   *Betula populifolia*

Small tree up to 30 feet high, leaves toothed, **triangular in outline with tapering tips,** bark close, not peeling, white with dark markings. Occasional in dry open areas and on ledges at low elevations. Flowers in May.

WHITE BIRCH   *Betula papyrifera*

Tree up to 60 feet high, leaves toothed, rounded at the base, **bark white, outer layers freely separating into thin strips.** Common in the hardwood forest at low elevations; at high elevations replaced by heart-leaved white birch. Flowers in May. The bark of this tree was used by Indians to make canoes. Peeling the bark leaves a permanent, unsightly scar.

HEART-LEAVED WHITE BIRCH   *Betula cordifolia*

Small tree or shrub, resembling white birch but **leaves heart-shaped at base and bark reddish-brown.** Common at medium and high elevations and in the alpine zone, where it occurs as a straggling shrub. Flowers May, June.

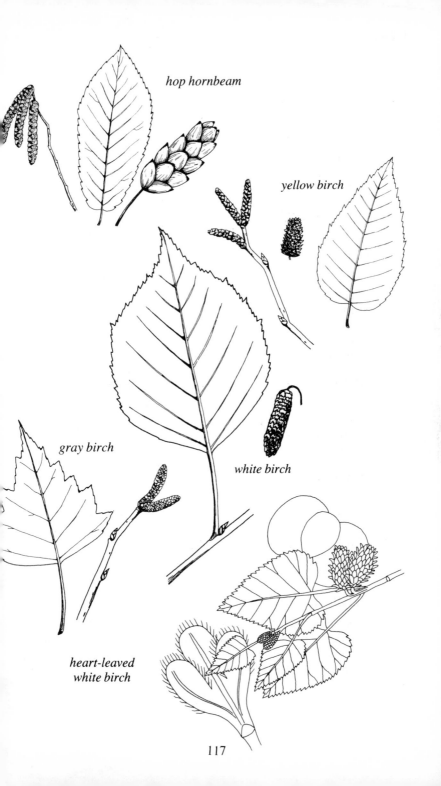

hop hornbeam

yellow birch

gray birch

white birch

heart-leaved
white birch

117

BEAKED HAZELNUT   *Corylus cornuta*

Straggling shrub up to 3 feet high, leaves 2 to 4 inches long, double toothed, **nut enclosed in a long, bristly, tubelike beak.** Occasional in thickets and borders of woods at low elevations. Flowers in April; fruits June to Aug. Nuts edible but quickly eaten by chipmunks.

MOUNTAIN BIRCH   *Betula minor*

Shrub up to 6 feet high, resembles heart-leaved white birch but leaves smaller, 1 to 2 inches long, **rounded or wedge-shaped at base,** catkins up to 2 inches long. Common in alpine ravines and alpine areas. Flowers in June, July. The following two birches also occur in the alpine zone, and it is not always easy to distinguish among the three.

ALPINE BIRCH   *Betula glandulosa*

Low or trailing shrub up to 2 feet high, leaves small, ¾ inch long, **round with rounded or scalloped teeth,** catkins less than 1 inch long. Frequent in alpine areas of Katahdin, the Presidential Range, and the Adirondacks, widespread in the Arctic. Flowers June, July.

NORTHERN BIRCH   *Betula borealis*

Shrub resembling mountain birch but **new twigs hairy.** Rare on Katahdin, more common in eastern Canada. Flowers in June, July.

ALDER   *Alnus rugosa*

Large shrub up to 16 feet high, usually growing in clumps, **leaves double toothed, pale beneath,** bark dark brown with whitish horizontal spots. Common in open wet areas at low elevations. Flowers in April. Alder is a favorite food of beavers and frequently used in beaver dams and houses.

GREEN   *Alnus crispa*
or MOUNTAIN ALDER

Shrub up to 6 feet high, **leaves finely and evenly toothed, green underside,** catkins on erect stalks, up to 1 inch long. Frequent along streams and in alpine ravines, ascending to the edge of the alpine area. Flowers May, June. The pistillate catkins are fragrant and remain on the plant all summer. Alders can fix atmospheric nitrogen. They are pioneer plants on gravels and landslides.

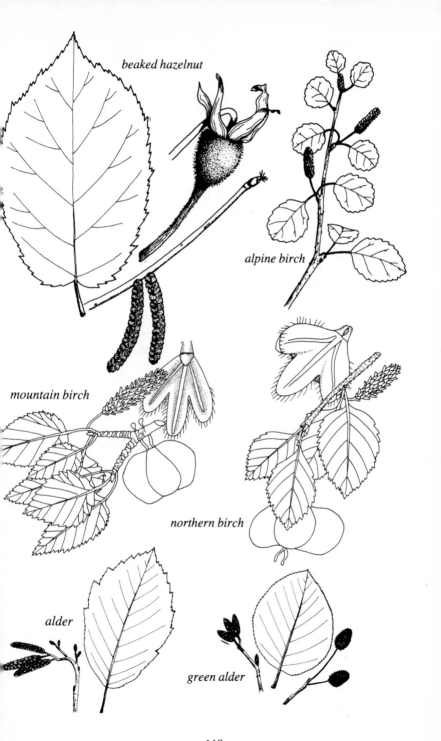

beaked hazelnut

alpine birch

mountain birch

northern birch

alder

green alder

119

TREES

MAPLE FAMILY

Trees and shrubs. All members of this family have leaves and twigs opposite on the stem, the leaves lobed. The fruit is a pair of winged seeds (keys) that separate and float through the air, spinning like a miniature propeller.

STRIPED MAPLE   *Acer pensylvanicum*

Tall shrub or slender tree up to 30 feet high, leaves **often large, up to 8 inches broad,** with 3 main lobes, **margin with small regularly spaced teeth,** bark smooth, greenish, **usually conspicuously streaked with black and white,** flowers yellow in long drooping clusters, fruit large winged seeds. Common in woods at low and medium elevations. Flowers in May; fruits in July.

SUGAR MAPLE   *Acer saccharum*

Large tree up to 100 feet high and 3 feet in diameter, leaves 5-lobed, **rounded between the lobes and without sharp teeth,** flowers yellow-green without petals, in drooping clusters, fruit a key. Common in hardwoods at low elevations. Flowers in May; fruits in June. The sap runs in March and April and is collected for maple sugar and syrup.

RED MAPLE   *Acer rubrum*

Tree up to 100 feet high and 3 feet in diameter, leaves 5-lobed **with sharp angles between the lobes and sharp irregular teeth,** flowers red or yellow, male and female on separate trees, fruit a key. Common at low and medium elevations, occuring higher on the slopes than sugar maple. Flowers in April; fruits in May, June. The sap can be used for syrup but is not as sweet as that of the sugar maple.

MOUNTAIN MAPLE   *Acer spicatum*

Shrub or occasionally small tree up to 20 feet, leaves resembling red maple's but **teeth scalloped with rounded margins,** bark smooth often mottled, flowers small, yellow, numerous in erect clusters up to 3 inches long, fruit a key. Common in woods at low and medium elevations. Flowers in mid-May, June; fruits July. In spite of its name it is not usually found high on mountain slopes.

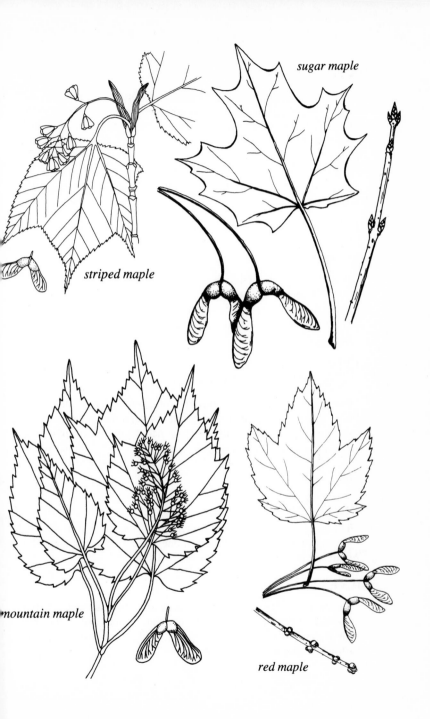

sugar maple

striped maple

mountain maple

red maple

121

WILLOW FAMILY

This family includes willows, which are all shrubs in the mountains, and poplars, which are trees. Pussy willows are the best known of the willows. The "pussies" are the silky catkins in the bud stage, which later expand and produce stamens and pistils. All of the trees and shrubs in this family have catkins and are most easily recognized in the spring when they flower. Willows are unusual in that the sexes are separate: a plant is either male or female (having stamens or pistils), but not both.

The willows in this group are restricted to the alpine zone.

DWARF WILLOW *Salix herbacea*

Dwarf shrub about 4 inches high with stem that is barely woody, leaves **1 inch long, nearly round,** small catkins ¼ inch long with reddish-brown seed pods. Occasional in mossy alpine areas on Washington and Katahdin, widespread in the Arctic. Flowers late June to August.

ALPINE *Salix uva-ursi*
or BEARBERRY WILLOW

Prostrate or trailing shrub, forming mats with a rather thick woody stem, leaves **lustrous-green above, pale beneath,** catkins small, silky in bud, lengthening to 1 inch. Common in alpine areas of Katahdin and the White Mountains, occasional in alpine areas of Vermont and New York, widespread in the Arctic. Flowers in late May to mid-June.

ARCTIC WILLOW *Salix arctophilia*

Trailing or low erect shrub 6 inches to 1 foot high, leaves **shiny above, pale beneath.** Occurs in one remote ravine on Katahdin, widespread in the Arctic. Flowers mid-June, July.

SILVER WILLOW *Salix argyrocarpa*

Shrub up to 4 feet high, leaves **silvery-silky beneath with glistening hairs.** Frequent near brooks in alpine ravines and alpine areas on Washington, more common in mountains of eastern Canada. Flowers June to early August.

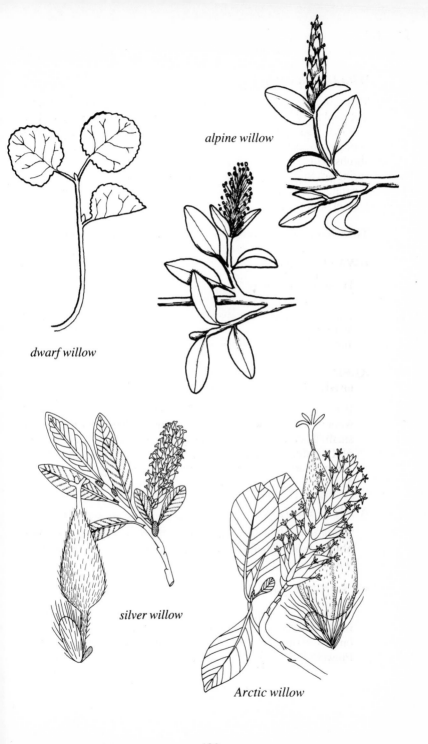

alpine willow

dwarf willow

silver willow

Arctic willow

TEA-LEAVED WILLOW   *Salix planifolia*

Similar to silver willow but leaves **pale beneath without hairs.** Frequent near brooks in alpine ravines and alpine areas of Washington and Katahdin, also in mountains of eastern Canada. Flowers June to early August.

The willows in this group are not alpine.

BALSAM WILLOW   *Salix pyrifolia*

Shrub up to 6 feet high, leaves toothed, **rather broad, up to 1½ inches wide,** rounded or slightly heart-shaped at base. Occasional in moist areas at low and medium elevations and at the lower edge of alpine ravines. Flowers mid-May, June. The crushed leaves have a faint odor of balsam.

STIFF WILLOW   *Salix rigida*

Shrub up to 6 feet high, leaves **narrow, finely toothed, pale beneath.** Frequent along banks of streams and in open moist places at low and medium elevations. Flowers May, June.

SHINY WILLOW   *Salix lucida*

Shrub up to 4 feet high, leaves finely toothed, **long and taper-pointed, upper surface shiny,** bright green on both sides. Occasional in wet places along streams at low elevations. Flowers May, June.

BEAKED WILLOW   *Salix bebbiana*

Shrub up to 6 feet high, **leaves pale and strongly veined beneath,** with no teeth or irregularly scattered teeth. Common in open areas at low elevations, occasional at medium elevations. Flowers May, June.

PUSSY WILLOW   *Salix discolor*

Shrub up to 6 feet, leaves with **few or no teeth, pale and whitish beneath.** Common in open areas at low elevations, occasionally higher. Flowers in April, May. This is the best known willow because of its silky flower buds, which appear in early spring.

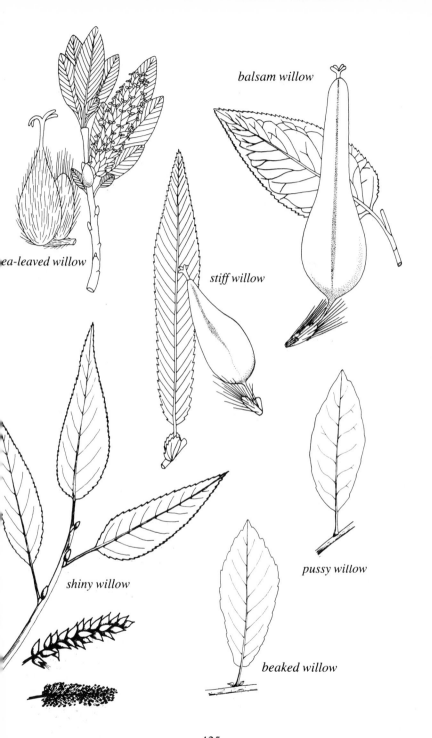

balsam willow

ea-leaved willow

stiff willow

shiny willow

pussy willow

beaked willow

SMALL-TOOTH ASPEN or POPLAR
Populus tremuloides

Tree up to 60 feet high, **stem of leaf flat, leaf finely toothed,** flower buds resembling pussy willows. Common in dry woods at low elevations. Flowers in April. Also called trembling aspen because the leaves flutter and turn in a light breeze.

LARGE-TOOTH ASPEN or POPLAR
Populus grandidentata

Tree up to 60 feet high, resembles the preceding but **teeth coarse and rather widely separated.** Common in dry woods at low elevations. Flowers mid-April, May.

DOGWOOD FAMILY

Shrubs and herbs. The shrubs are all similar in appearance, with strongly veined leaves and flat clusters of small flowers.

RED OSIER DOGWOOD
Cornus stolonifera

Shrub up to 6 feet high, leaves opposite without teeth, strongly veined, smooth beneath, new and second year stems deep red, flowers white, fruit red or lead-colored, hard. Frequent at low elevations, often in wet places. Flowers in June; fruits July to Sept.

ROUND-LEAVED DOGWOOD
Cornus rugosa

Shrub up to 6 feet high, resembles red osier dogwood but leaves **nearly round, up to 4 inches across, wooly underneath,** flowers white, fruit blue. Occasional in rocky woods or on talus slopes at low elevations. Flowers in June; fruits July to Sept.

ALTERNATE-LEAVED DOGWOOD
Cornus alternifolia

Shrub up to 8 feet high, leaves alternate on the stem, **crowded at the tip of the branch,** flowers white, fruit bluish-black. Frequent in woods at low elevations. Flowers in June; fruits July to Sept.

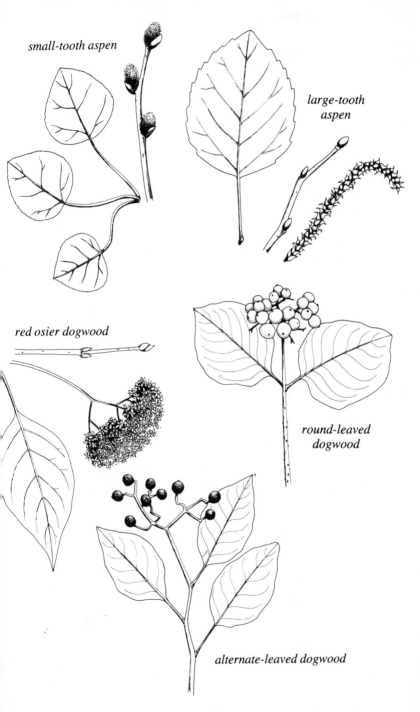

small-tooth aspen

large-tooth aspen

red osier dogwood

round-leaved dogwood

alternate-leaved dogwood

127

TREES

ROSE FAMILY

Trees, shrubs, and herbs. All have conspicuous flowers with 5 petals and numerous stamens and pistils, resembling an apple flower but smaller.

MEADOWSWEET *Spiraea latifolia*

Shrub up to 3 feet high with tough stem, **flowers small, white, borne in dense conical clusters,** fruit a hard dry pod. Common in open areas from low elevations to the edge of the alpine zone. Flowers July to Sept. At high elevations the flower clusters are short and compact.

HARDHACK or STEEPLEBUSH *Spiraea tomentosa*

Shrub up to 3 feet high, leaves **densely wooly underneath, flowers deep pink.** Occasional in open areas at low elevations, sometimes higher. Flowers Aug., Sept.

BLACK CHOKEBERRY *Aronia melanocarpa*

Shrub up to 5 feet high, leaves up to 2 inches long, finely toothed, leaves and leafstalks **hairless,** flowers ½ inch across with **5 white or pinkish petals,** fruit a dark purple berry, ¼ inch in diameter. Occasional at low and medium elevations in swamps and on dry ledges. Flowers in June; fruits in July. Fruit puckery to taste.

PURPLE CHOKEBERRY *Aronia prunifolia*

Closely resembles the preceding but lower leaf surfaces and leafstalks **slightly hairy underneath.** Occurs in similar habitats. Not illustrated.

MOUNTAIN ASH *Sorbus americana*

Large shrub or small tree up to 20 feet high, leaves **compound with 11 to 17 leaflets, flowers small, white, very numerous in large flat clusters,** fruit a bright red berry, ¼ inch in diameter. Common in open and rocky areas at all elevations, reaching the edge of the alpine area. Flowers in June; fruits in Aug. The fruit is inedible to humans, though a favorite of birds. Though flowers or fruit readily identify this shrub, they often do not develop. In that event the large compound leaf is a good field mark.

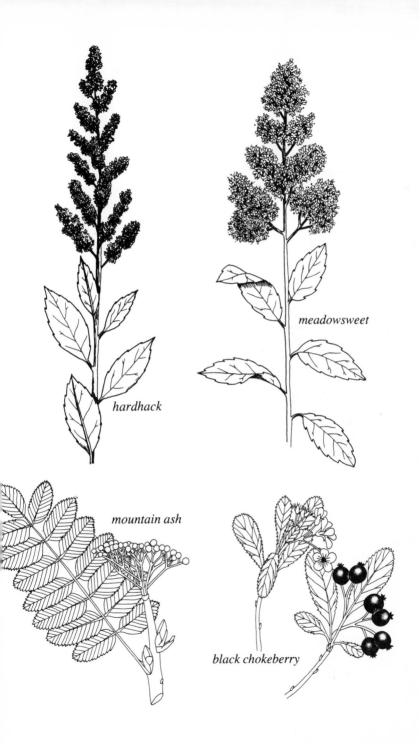

hardhack

meadowsweet

mountain ash

black chokeberry

NORTHERN MOUNTAIN ASH   *Sorbus decora*

Closely resembling the preceding but leaflets a little shorter and **blue-green** above. Occurs in similar habitats. Not illustrated.

EARLY SHADBUSH   *Amelanchier laevis*

Shrub or small tree up to 30 feet high, leaves finely and evenly toothed, **heart-shaped at the base,** flowers white with 5 narrow petals in **showy nodding clusters up to 2 inches long,** fruit a red berry with a flower resembling a small apple blossom. Common at low elevations in swamps and open woods. Flowers in May; fruits June, July. The sweet fruits are edible. It gets its name from the fact that it blooms in May when the shad used to run.

MOUNTAIN SHADBUSH   *Amelanchier bartramiana*

Small shrub 2 to 7 feet high, resembles the preceding but leaves **narrow and tapering at the base,** flowers 1 to 4 **arising from the same point on the stem.** Occasional in bogs at low elevations, more common on upper slopes and ascending to alpine areas. Flowers in May; fruits June, July.

SHRUBBY CINQUEFOIL   *Potentilla fruticosa*

Small shrub up to 3 feet high, leaves **compound with 5 to 7 leaflets,** flowers **yellow,** fruit small and dry. Occasional on ledges or in open wet areas at low elevations, rare in alpine ravines. Flowers July, Aug.

RASPBERRY   *Rubus idaeus*

Shrub up to 2 feet high, the canes flowering the second year and then dying, leaves compound, stem **bristly and with some prickles,** flowers white, small clusters, fruit a mass of small red berries. Common in open areas at low and medium, elevations, occasional in alpine ravines. Flowers in June; fruits July, Aug. The fruits are edible and very good. They are a favorite food of bears.

BLACKBERRY   *Rubus canadensis*

In aspect resembling the raspberry but taller and with scattered sharp prickles, flowers white, **fruit black.** Frequent in open woods mostly at low elevations. Flowers in June; fruits July, Aug. Other species of blackberries may be found in the mountains, some of which are much more prickly than this one. Some have good fruits.

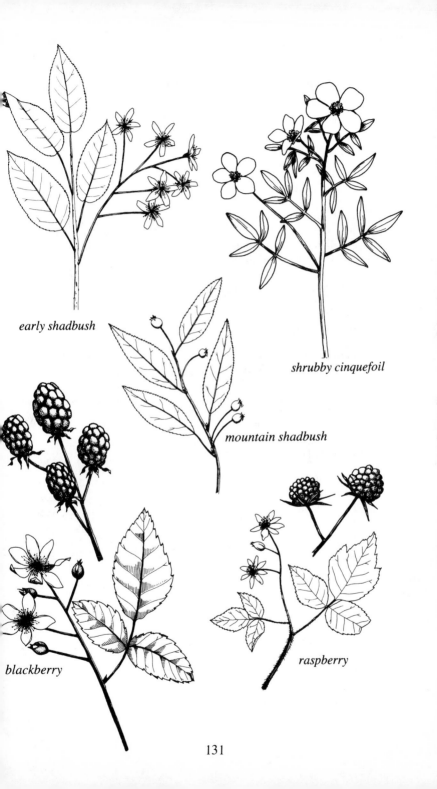

early shadbush

shrubby cinquefoil

mountain shadbush

blackberry

raspberry

131

PURPLE-FLOWERING RASPBERRY   *Rubus odoratus*

Shrub up to 3 feet high, leaves 3 to 5 inches broad, **lobed, resembling maple,** stem without prickles, **flowers showy, purple,** more than 1 inch across, fruit resembling raspberry but dry and tasteless. Occasional in rocky woods or near ledges at low elevations. Flowers June to Aug.

RED CHERRY   *Prunus pensylvanica*

Small tree up to 30 feet high, leaves tapering to a point, finely toothed, **teeth tipped with small knobbed hairs, bark thin, reddish-brown,** flowers white with round petals, **all rising from the same point on the stem,** fruit red with a large stone. Common in open and lumbered areas at low and medium elevations ascending to alpine ravines. Flowers May, June; fruits July, Aug. The fruit is edible but sour with little pulp. Much of it is eaten by birds.

BLACK CHERRY   *Prunus serotina*

Tree up to 50 feet high, leaves larger and broader than red cherry, **teeth not as fine and without knobbed hairs,** bark on old trees scaly, flowers white in **elongate clusters up to 4 inches long,** fruit black with a stone. Occasional in hardwoods or open areas at low elevations. Flowers May, June; fruits Aug. Sept. The cherries have a good flavor.

CHOKE CHERRY   *Prunus virginiana*

Shrub up to 15 feet high, leaves 1 to 3 inches long with fine teeth, **broadest above the middle,** flowers similar to black cherry, fruit black. Common in open areas and on ledges at low and medium elevations. Flowers May; fruits Aug. to Oct. The raw fruits are puckery but can be made into a good jelly. Leaf illustrated with black cherry.

purple-flowering raspberry

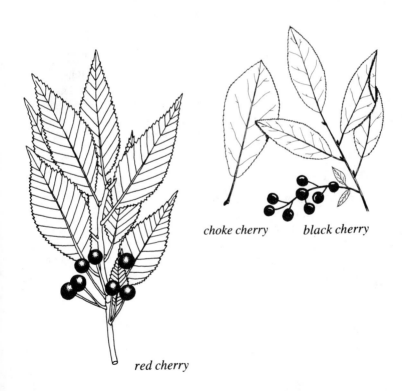

choke cherry   *black cherry*

red cherry

SAXIFRAGE FAMILY

Shrubs and herbs. The shrubs have lobed leaves resembling maple leaves but smaller. They produce edible fruits.

PRICKLY GOOSEBERRY   *Ribes cynosbati*

Shrub up to 2 feet high, leaves less than 2 inches long, **lobed and toothed, stem with scattered thin spines,** flowers small, green; fruit a berry armed with stiff prickles. Occasional in rocky woods at low elevations. Flowers in May; fruits in July.

SKUNK CURRANT   *Ribes glandulosum*

Shrub up to 2 feet high, leaves up to 2 inches long, lobed, with a **distinct odor of skunk when crushed,** flowers white to pinkish, fruit a **red berry, ¼ inch in diameter, covered with small hairs.** Frequent in wet or rocky woods at all elevations, reaching the edge of the alpine zone. Flowers in May; fruits in July. The berries have a slight odor of skunk but are not unpleasant to eat.

BRISTLY BLACK CURRANT   *Ribes lacustre*

Shrub up to 2 feet high, leaves up to 3 inches long, **deeply lobed and cut-toothed,** stem clothed with **numerous bristles and some prickles,** flowers green, fruit a **black berry,** ¼ inch in diameter, covered with bristles. Frequent in damp woods from low elevations to alpine ravines. Flowers May, June; fruits July to Sept. The berries are sweet and tasty.

RED CURRANT   *Ribes triste*

Straggling or erect shrub up to 2 feet high, leaves up to 3 inches long, with **lobes and sides nearly parallel,** flowers purple to yellowish, fruit red, small and hard. Occasional in wet woods from low elevations to alpine ravines. Flowers May to July; fruits June to Aug. The fruits are not poisonous but neither are they succulent.

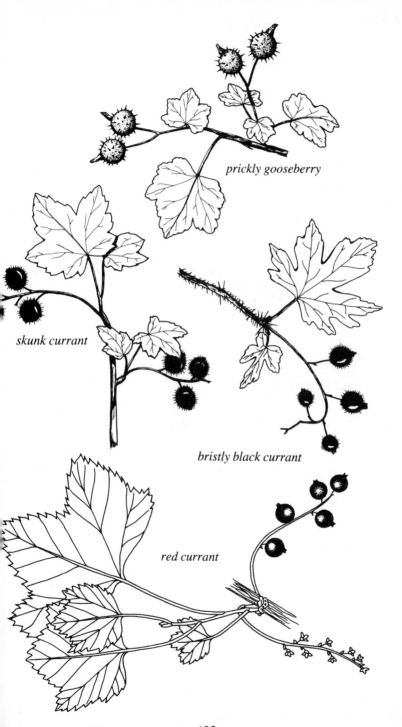

prickly gooseberry

skunk currant

bristly black currant

red currant

TREES

CROWBERRY FAMILY

BLACK CROWBERRY   *Empetrum nigrum*

Trailing shrub forming mats, **small needlelike evergreen leaves,** less than ½ inch long, many of them **bent back,** pointing toward the bottom of the stem, flowers very small, fruit a black berry. Common in alpine areas and often on rocky peaks of lower mountains. Flowers mid-May to mid-June; fruits July, Aug. The berries are edible but of poor quality.

PURPLE CROWBERRY   *Empetrum atropupureum*

Shrub resembling black crowberry but leaves **not bent back,** new leaves wooly underneath, **new branchlets white and wooly,** fruit red or purple-black. Frequent in alpine areas of mountains of Maine and New Hampshire, more common on rocky summits of lower mountains. Flowers June; fruits July to Sept. In spite of the name the berries are seldom eaten by crows.

HOLLY FAMILY

BLACK ALDER   *Ilex verticillata*

Shrub 3 to 10 feet high, leaves 1 to 3 inches long with coarse rounded teeth, flowers **small, white, with 6 to 8 petals** seated directly on the stem, fruit a scarlet berry about ¼ inch in diameter. Common in thickets and swamps at low elevations. Flowers in June; fruits July to Oct. The black alder is not related to the alder of the birch family. The berry is not edible.

MOUNTAIN HOLLY   *Nemopanthus mucronatus*

Branching shrub up to 9 feet high, leaves 1 to 2 inches long, thin, **lacking teeth, pale beneath,** flowers small, yellowish, on thin stalks, fruit a crimson berry. Common in swamps and moist woods at low and medium elevations. Flowers in June; fruits in July, Aug. The berry is not edible.

purple crowberry

black crowberry

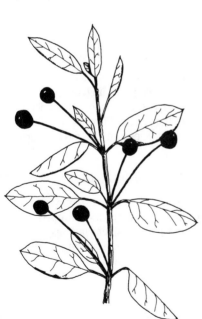

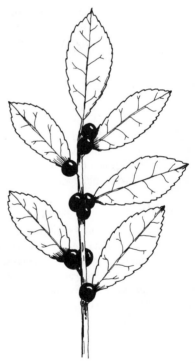

mountain holly

black alder

TREES

HEATH FAMILY

Shrubs or herbs, many of them evergreen, flowers with 5 or occasionally 4 petals, stamens as many or twice as many as the petals. The flowers are white or colored, and plants of this family are the most attractive and most visible flowers in the alpine zone in June.

LEATHERLEAF — *Chamaedaphne calyculata*

Low branching shrub up to 2 feet high, leaves **tough and leathery, evergreen, covered with small dots giving them a scurfy appearance,** flowers small, white, hanging in lines under the stem. Common in bogs or swamps, mostly at low elevations but occasionally near mountaintops. Flowers late April, mid-May.

LABRADOR TEA — *Ledum groenlandicum*

Shrub up to 2 feet high, leaves evergreen, narrow with inrolled margin, **underside covered with dense rusty wool,** flowers small, white in flat clusters, fruit a small pod. Common in bogs at all elevations and in moist or peaty areas in the alpine zone. Flowers in June; fruits July to Sept. The steeped leaves make a tea of poor quality.

LAPLAND ROSEBAY — *Rhododendron lapponicum*

Low shrub up to 1 foot high forming mats, leaves thick, evergreen, less than 1 inch long. **flowers showy, purple, 1 inch across,** fruit a small dry pod. Common in alpine areas of Katahdin, Presidential Range, and Adirondacks, also in the Arctic. Flowers late May to mid-June; fruits June to Sept. This is one of the most colorful flowers in the alpine zone.

RHODORA — *Rhododendron canadense*

Shrub up to 3 feet high, leaves up to 2 inches long, not evergreen, hairy underneath, flowers **rose-purple, somewhat 2-lipped, appearing before the leaves,** fruit a pod. Frequent in bogs and on rocky slopes at low elevations, occasionally ascending to alpine areas. Flowers May; fruits June to Sept. When in flower, this shrub forms masses of color.

Lapland rosebay

leatherleaf

Labrador tea

rhodora

139

ALPINE AZALEA
Loiseleuria procumbens

Dwarf shrub up to 6 inches high forming mats, leaves evergreen, thick, about ½ inch long, **flowers pink, about ¼ inch across,** fruit a small pod, ⅛ inch long. Common in alpine areas of Katahdin and Washington, also in the Arctic. Flowers late May to mid-June. The flowers are small but often in masses, so this is another colorful shrub in early June. In spite of its name, this is not an azalea.

SHEEP LAUREL
Kalmia angustifolia

Shrub up to 3 feet high, leaves mostly opposite, **crowded on the stem,** evergreen, flowers **deep pink, in clusters among the leaves** below the top of the stem, fruit a small pod. Frequent in swamps and rocky areas at low and medium elevations. Flowers in June. The leaves are considered poisonous to sheep and probably likewise to humans.

PALE LAUREL
Kalmia polifolia

Shrub up to 2 feet high, leaves evergreen, opposite, **whitish beneath with inrolled margins,** flowers deep pink in a **showy cluster at the top of the stem.** Frequent in bogs at low elevations, occasional in boggy areas in the alpine zone. Flowers mid-May, June.

MOUNTAIN HEATH
Phyllodoce caerulea

Dwarf shrub up to 6 inches high, leaves evergreen, numerous, needle-shaped, up to ½ inch long, flowers **light purple, urn-shaped, ¼ inch long, on nodding stems,** fruit a small dry pod. Occasional on Washington in the alpine zone, rare on Katahdin and Franconia Range, widespread in the Arctic. Flowers mid-June. This plant often grows in late snow areas.

ANDROMEDA
Andromeda glaucophylla

Shrub up to 2 feet high, leaves narrow, evergreen, **pale bluish-green above, whitish beneath,** flowers small, white, urn-shaped, in small clusters, fruit a round pod. Occasional in bogs at low elevations and in one alpine ravine on Katahdin. Flowers in May. When not in flower it resembles pale laurel except that the leaves are alternate.

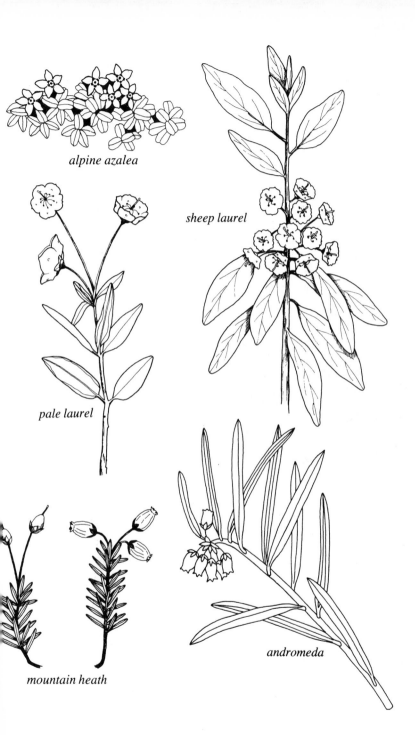

alpine azalea

sheep laurel

pale laurel

mountain heath

andromeda

141

MOSS PLANT
Cassiope hypnoides

Dwarf shrub up to 3 inches high, leaves **evergreen and mosslike,** flowers small, white, **nodding, bell-shaped with 4 red sepals forming a cross at the top,** fruit a small round pod. Occasional in mossy and late snow areas on Washington and Katahdin, widespread in the Arctic. Flowers in mid-June. When not in flower the plant could easily be mistaken for a moss.

SNOWBERRY
Gaultheria hispidula

Trailing matted shrub with barely woody stems, leaves **small, about ¼ inch long, nearly round, evergreen,** flowers small and difficult to see, **fruit a white berry.** Frequent in mossy woods, especially coniferous woods from low and medium elevations to the edge of the alpine area. Flowers May, June. The berry is edible, mildly acidic and of good flavor.

ALPINE BEARBERRY
Arctostaphylos alpina

Trailing shrub up to 6 inches high, leaves up to ½ inch long with a **network of veins giving the leaves a wrinkled appearance,** flowers small, white, urn-shaped, fruit a purple berry. Common in the alpine area of Katahdin, rare on Washington, widespread in the Arctic. Flowers early June; fruits July, Aug. The berry is edible but the fruits seldom develop.

BLACK HUCKLEBERRY
Gaylussacia baccata

Shrub up to 3 feet high, leaves with both surfaces **clammy with small resinous dots,** flowers small, white, urn-shaped, fruit a blue berry with 10 seeds. Occasional on ledges and bare summits of lower mountains. Flowers mid-May to June; fruits July to Sept. The fruit is edible, sweet and of good flavor.

BOG BILBERRY
Vaccinium uliginosum

Shrub up to 1 foot high, leaves up to ½ inch long, **oval or nearly round, pale, bluish-green,** flowers white, urn-shaped, berries blue resembling blueberries but not in clusters. Common in alpine areas and on rocky summits of lower mountains. Flowers in June; fruits July to Sept. The berry is edible with a flavor slightly different from the blueberry's.

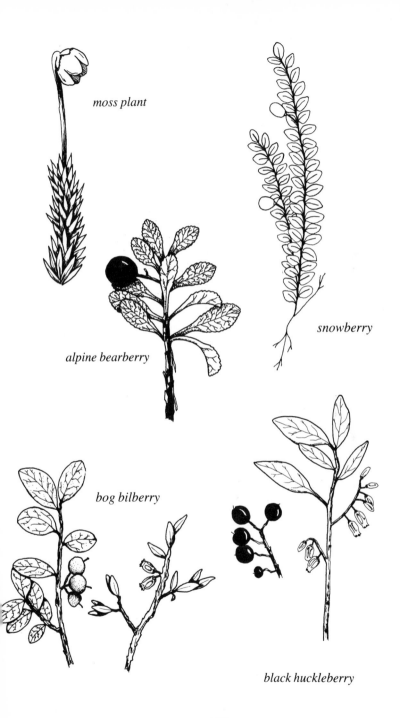

moss plant

snowberry

alpine bearberry

bog bilberry

black huckleberry

DWARF BILBERRY   *Vaccinium cespitosum*

Dwarf shrub, depressed or ascending to 6 inches, resembles low blueberry, leaves toothed, **broadest above the middle,** flowers white, fruit blue, **borne singly or in clusters of 2 or 3.** Common in alpine areas, occasional on bare summits of lower mountains. Flowers in June; fruits July to Sept. Berries edible.

LOW BLUEBERRY   *Vaccinium angustifolium*

Shrub up to 1 foot high, leaves about 1 inch long, narrow, **lined with fine teeth,** flowers white, urn-shaped, fruit a blue or less often a black berry. Common on ledges and in open areas from low elevations to the alpine zone. Flowers May, June; fruits July, Aug. The berries are edible and of excellent quality.

SOUR-TOP BLUEBERRY   *Vaccinium myrtilloides*

Resembles the preceding, but **leaves without teeth.** Common in open areas from low to high elevations but not in the alpine zone.

MOUNTAIN CRANBERRY   *Vaccinium vitis-idaea*

Low creeping shrub up to 6 inches high, leaves ½ inch long, **thick, shiny with a waxy covering, evergreen,** flowers pink, urn-shaped, fruit a dark red berry ¼ inch in diameter. Common in alpine areas and on rocky summits of lower mountains in Maine, New Hampshire, and Vermont. Flowers June; fruits Aug., Sept. The raw berries are not very good but make an excellent sauce when cooked.

SMALL CRANBERRY   *Oxycoccus palustris*

Creeping and forking shrub less than 1 foot high, forming mats. Leaves **less than ¼ inch long, whitish beneath,** with inrolled margins, flowers white or pink, **fruit a red berry about ¼ inch in diameter.** Frequent in bogs at low elevations, occasionally higher, up to the alpine zone. Flowers June; fruits Aug. to Oct. The berries make an excellent sauce when cooked.

LARGE CRANBERRY   *Oxycoccus macrocarpon*

Similar to the preceding but leaves ½ **inch long** and berries larger. Occasional in bogs at low elevations. Cultivated cranberries are derived from this species.

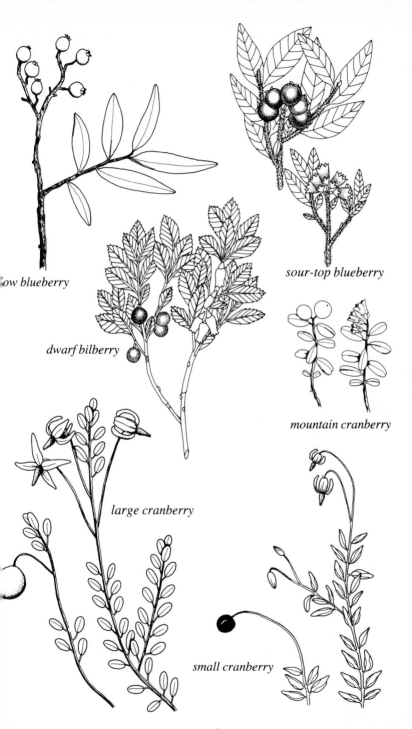

ow blueberry

sour-top blueberry

dwarf bilberry

mountain cranberry

large cranberry

small cranberry

TREES

HONEYSUCKLE FAMILY

Shrubs and a few herbs. All have opposite leaves and conspicuous white or pale yellow flowers, often showy.

BUSH HONEYSUCKLE *Diervilla Lonicera*

Low shrub up to 3 feet high, leaves **opposite, sharply toothed,** 2 to 4 inches long, flowers funnel-shaped, **yellow in clusters of 2 to 10,** fruit a slender pod about ½ inch long. Common in dry or rocky woods and on talus slopes at low and medium elevations, ascending to alpine ravines. Flowers June, July; fruits July to Sept.

MOUNTAIN FLY HONEYSUCKLE *Lonicera villosa*

Shrub up to 3 feet high. Leaves opposite, **short, up to 1 inch long,** often hairy, **leaf stalk very short,** flowers in pairs, **pale yellow,** about ½ inch long, fruit a blue berry. Occasional in bogs and on slopes, frequent in wet or boggy areas in ravines and alpine areas of Washington and Katahdin. Flowers in June, mid-July; fruits July to Sept. The berry is edible.

AMERICAN FLY HONEYSUCKLE *Lonicera canadensis*

Straggling shrub up to 4 feet high, resembles the preceding but leaves larger, **about 2 inches long on short stems** and with no hairs, flowers **pale yellow, 3/4 inch long,** fruit a blue berry. Frequent in woods at low and medium elevations. Flowers May to mid-June; fruits July to Sept. The fruits seldom ripen.

WITHEROD *Viburnum cassinoides*

Shrub 3 to 10 feet high forming dense thickets in wet places, leaves opposite, **loosely toothed or toothless,** flowers small, white, in **flat clusters 2 to 4 inches across,** fruit ½ inch long, pulpy with a stone, whitish when young, turning dark blue. Frequent in swamps and open areas from low to high elevations. Flowers in June; fruits Aug., Sept. The name comes from withe, a slender flexible branch used in basket-making.

MAPLE-LEAVED VIBURNUM *Viburnum acerifolium*

Shrub up to 6 feet high. Leaves opposite, **3-lobed resembling a maple leaf, soft downy beneath,** flowers small, white, in a flat cluster **1½ to 3½ inches across,** fruit purple-black. Frequent in dry or rocky woods at low elevations. Flowers in June; fruits July to Sept. The fruits usually do not mature.

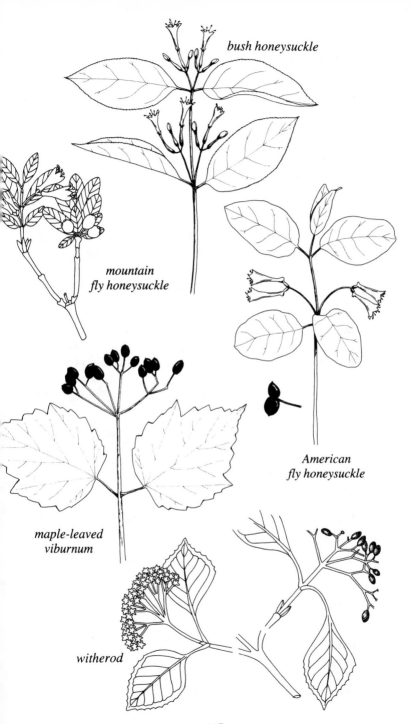

bush honeysuckle

mountain
fly honeysuckle

American
fly honeysuckle

maple-leaved
viburnum

witherod

147

SQUASHBERRY — *Viburnum edule*

Shrub up to 6 feet high somewhat resembling the preceding, leaves opposite, either lobed or with 3 short lobes, **smooth underneath,** flowers small, white in clusters **less than 1½ inch across,** fruits yellow or orange. Occasional in moist woods or swamps at low elevations, becoming more common in the alpine zone in wet places. The fruits are said to make a good jam but they are difficult to collect in quantity. Flowers June, July.

HIGHBUSH CRANBERRY — *Viburnum trilobum*

Shrub up to 12 feet high, leaves opposite, 3-lobed, flowers white, **of 2 kinds, the outer showy and large, 1 inch across, the inner small.** Fruit red, pulpy with a stone. Occasional in moist or swampy woods at low and medium elevations. Flowers in June; fruits July to Oct. The acidic fruit makes a good jelly.

HOBBLEBUSH — *Viburnum alnifolium*

Straggling shrub 3 to 8 feet high, leaves opposite, **nearly round, finely toothed, heart-shaped at the base,** rather large, flowers white, **of 2 kinds, the outer large and showy, the inner small.** Fruit hard and red. Common in woods at low and medium elevations. Flowers in May; fruits Aug. to Oct. Hobblebush where deer browse becomes stunted, with small atypical leaves.

ELDER or ELDERBERRY — *Sambucus canadensis*

Shrub up to 10 feet high, leaves opposite, **compound with 5 to 11 sharply toothed leaflets,** flowers small, white, **very numerous in flat or slightly rounded clusters,** fruit a small black berry. Frequent in open areas at low or occasionally medium elevations. Flowers mid-June to mid-July; fruits Aug., Sept. The ripe berries make excellent jelly and wine.

RED-BERRIED ELDER — *Sambucus pubens*

Shrub up to 10 feet high, resembling elderberry but **flowers and fruits in egg-shaped or pyramidal clusters,** fruit a red berry. Frequent in open areas and on ledges at low elevations ascending to alpine ravines. Flowers in May; fruits in July. Many of the berries do not ripen and are inedible.

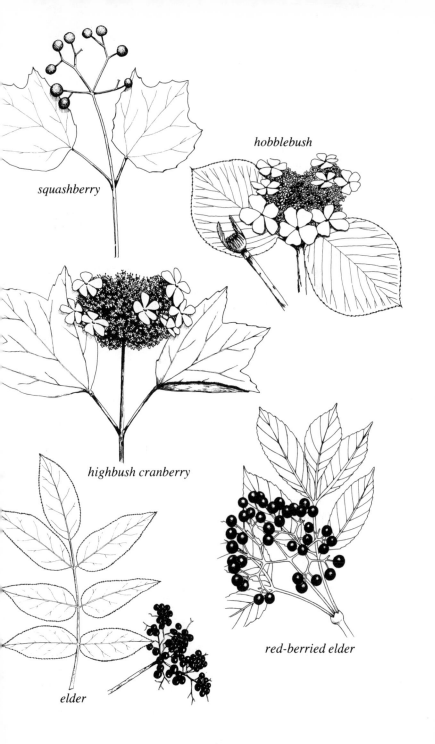

squashberry

hobblebush

highbush cranberry

elder

red-berried elder

149

TREES

WAXMYRTLE FAMILY

SWEET GALE *Myrica gale*

Spreading shrub up to 4 feet high, leaves narrow, **broadest near the tip and with a few scattered teeth at the tip,** flowers in short scaly catkins. Common in bogs and on edges of ponds at low elevations. Flowers in May. The crushed leaves and catkins have a pleasant fragrance.

YEW FAMILY

AMERICAN YEW *Taxus canadensis*

Low straggling evergreen shrub up to 3 feet high. Needles **soft, yellowish-green beneath,** fruit a red berry with a hard poisonous seed in the middle. Frequent in woods at low elevations. In winter deer browse on yew, and bitten-off twigs can be seen in summer.

sweet gale

American yew

Ferns and Fern Allies

The plants described in this section reproduce by spores instead of seeds. A spore is as small as a dust particle; a single spore can only be studied under a microscope. The spore cases that contain the spores are usually easy to see and are therefore an aid in identification.

Organization

There are twenty-two ferns included in this guide, many of them common though some you are unlikely to see. The fern allies include many species of clubmoss, which are not true mosses.

Botanical Terms

The "leaf" of a fern is called a **frond**. The main segments are the **pinnae** (singular, **pinna**). These in turn may be divided into **pinnules**, which in some ferns are further divided into **lobes**. The reproductive spore cases are clustered into **fruit dots**, which are usually borne on the back of the pinnae but are sometimes on separate stalks. It is helpful in identifying ferns to look at the back of the fronds and notice the shape and arrangement of the fruit dots.

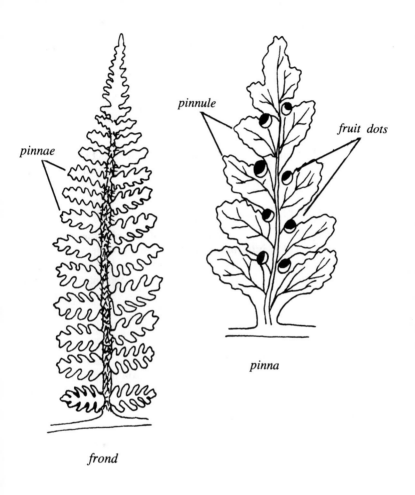

pinnule

pinnae

fruit dots

pinna

frond

Entries

Each entry includes a general description of the plant and where it is likely to be found. The most distinguishing characteristic of ferns and fern allies is their spore cases, which in ferns are clustered into fruit dots. Particular attention should be paid to descriptions of these.

FERNS

CINNAMON FERN
Osmunda cinnamomea

Large fern up to 5 feet high, the spore cases borne on **separate dense woolly stalks,** soon wilting. Pinnae with **small woolly tufts** at the base on the underside. Common in swamps and woods at low and medium elevations.

INTERRUPTED FERN
Osmunda Claytoniana

Resembles cinnamon fern but with spore cases borne on **small blackish pinnae near the middle of the frond.** Pinnae **bluish-green** and lacking woolly tufts. Common in swamps and wet woods at low and medium elevations.

HAY-SCENTED FERN
Dennstaedtia punctilobula

Frond up to 2 feet high, **pinnae divided into pinnules which are further divided into lobes.** Fruit dots small on the edges of the lobes. Common in open and lumbered areas at low elevations and occasionally up to 4000 feet. The crushed fronds have a pleasant odor suggesting new-mown hay.

BRAKE FERN
or BRACKEN
Pteridium aquilinum

Large fern up to 4 feet tall **with the main blade spreading horizontally in 3 parts.** Fruit dots small, on the partly recurved margins of the pinnules. Common in dry woods at low elevations and occasionally up to 4000 feet. The new young stalks up to 8 inches high are edible when cooked.

MAIDENHAIR FERN
Adiantum pedatum

Frond up to 2 feet high with a **black stem** forking at summit into recurving branches, **pinnules pale green and graceful.** Fruit dots on the margins, inconspicuous. Occasional in rich woods at low elevations, common in Vermont.

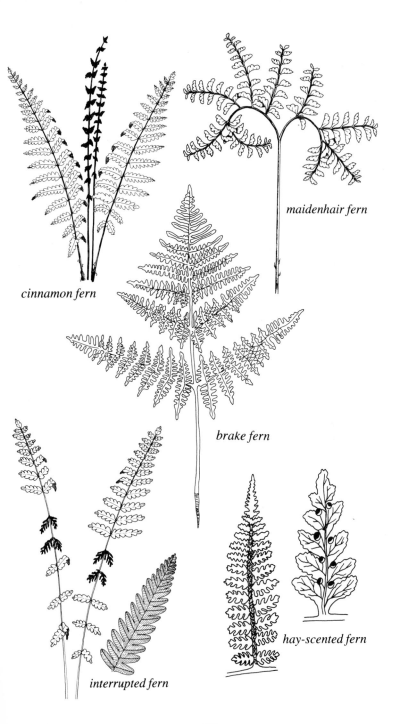

cinnamon fern

maidenhair fern

brake fern

interrupted fern

hay-scented fern

POLYPODY   *Polypodium virginianum*

Low fern up to 1 foot high, evergreen, frond divided into pinnae, but these **not divided into pinnules.** Fruit dots round near the margins of the pinnae. Frequent in rocky woods at low elevations and near the summit of Mansfield. This fern often grows on boulders.

GREEN SPLEENWORT   *Asplenium viride*

Small fern up to 4 inches high with a narrow frond up to ½ inch broad, **stem green.** Fruit dots conspicuous and occupying most of the pinna. Rare on mountain ledges and cliffs in Vermont.

MAIDENHAIR SPLEENWORT   *Asplenium trichomanes*

Resembling the preceding but somewhat larger, up to 8 inches high, forming dense tufts, **stem purple-brown and shiny.** Occasional on ledges and cliffs at low elevations.

LADY FERN   *Athyrium Filix-femina*

Frond up to 5 feet high divided into pinnae and pinnules, with the pinnules lobed or toothed, **stem with black scales at the base.** Fruit dots covering the backs of the pinnules. Common in dry areas at low elevations, less common on higher slopes and in alpine ravines.

SILVERY SPLEENWORT   *Athyrium thelypteroides*

Frond up to 4 feet high, pinnae deeply lobed. **Fruit dots in lines and silvery.** Frequent in hardwoods at low elevations.

RUSTY WOODSIA   *Woodsia ilvensis*

Low tufted fern up to 1 foot high, lower part of **stem chaffy and surrounded by dark bases of old stems.** Fruit dots somewhat hairy and covering the backs of the pinnules. Frequent on dry ledges at low elevations, occasionally up to alpine ravines.

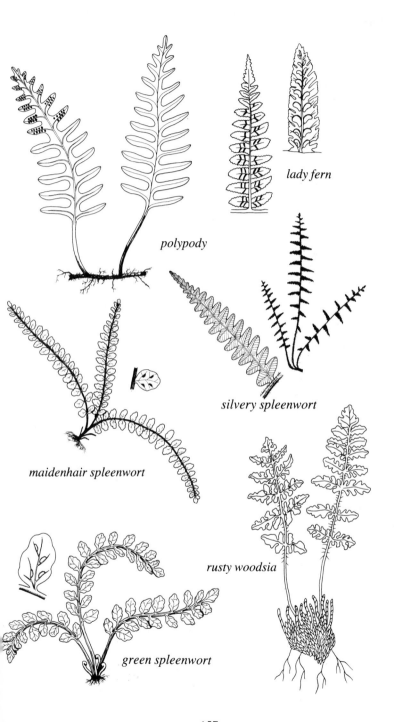

polypody

lady fern

silvery spleenwort

maidenhair spleenwort

rusty woodsia

green spleenwort

157

NORTHERN WOODSIA   *Woodsia alpina*

Resembling rusty woodsia but smaller and more delicate, **stem smooth without chaff.** Fruit dots on the margins of the pinnae. Occasional on mountain ledges and cliffs in Maine and Vermont.

SMOOTH WOODSIA   *Woodsia glabella*

Low, up to 6 inches high, forming small tufts 1 inch across at the base, **bases of old stems crowded around the new ones,** frond smooth without chaff. Rare on mountain ledges and cliffs, more common in Vermont.

FRAGILE BLADDERFERN   *Cystopteris fragilis*

Low **delicate fern** up to 1 foot high, frond divided into **pinnae and pinnules which are often further divided.** Fruit dots round and prominent. Frequent on ledges and cliffs at low elevations, also near the summits of Mansfield and Camel's Hump.

BEECH FERN   *Phelypteris phegopteris*

Frond up to 1 foot high, **triangular in shape,** ⅔ as broad as long, **2 lower pinnae projecting forward and downward.** Common in open woods at low elevations, occasional in grassy areas in the alpine zone.

NEW YORK FERN   *Thelypteris noveboracensis*

Frond up to 2 feet high, becoming **narrow at the base with widely spaced and increasingly smaller pinnae.** Common in dry woods at low elevations.

OAK FERN   *Gymnocarpium dryopteris*

Low delicate fern up to 1 foot high, frond **horizontal and triangular, divided into 3 main parts,** resembling a small brake fern. Common in hardwoods at low elevations, occasional near mountaintops.

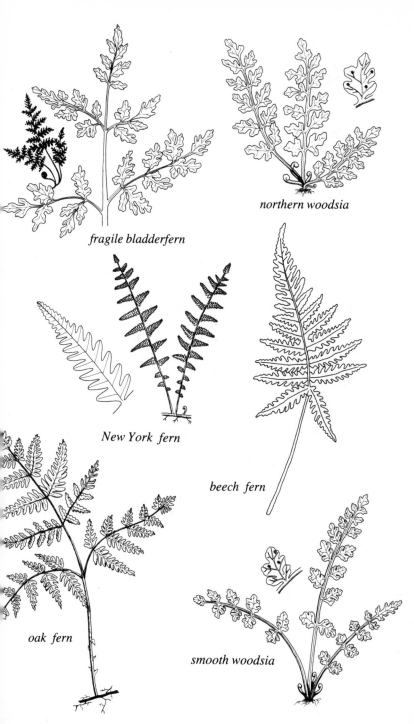

fragile bladderfern

northern woodsia

New York fern

beech fern

oak fern

smooth woodsia

FERNS

SPINY   *Dryopteris austriaca*
or SPINULOSE WOODFERN

Frond up to 4 feet high, **finely cut into pinnae and pinnules which are often further divided, stem with brown scales at the base,** which distinguishes it from the somewhat similar lady fern. Fruit dots round near the center of the pinnules. A common and characteristic plant of the evergreen woods at all elevations and in the alpine area. The fronds are evergreen.

MARGINAL SHIELDFERN   *Dryopteris marginalis*

Frond up to 3 feet high, **evergreen,** pinnules thick, blue-green. Fruit dots round on the **margins of the pinnules.** Common in woods at low elevations, occasionally higher on the slopes.

FRAGRANT FERN   *Dryopteris fragrans*

Fronds up to 8 inches high, **surrounded by dry curled old fronds,** stem with brown scales. Fruit dots covering the backs of the pinnules. Rare on ledges and cliffs at low elevations, in Vermont fairly common on Mansfield and Camel's Hump at all elevations.

CHRISTMAS FERN   *Polystichum acrostichoides*

Fronds up to 2 feet high, evergreen, **pinnae nearly separate from main stem, attached by a short stalk.** Fruit dots on small, shriveled upper pinnae. Common in woods at low elevations.

BRAUN'S HOLLY FERN   *Polystichum braunii*

Frond up to 2 feet high, divided into pinnae and pinnules which have **bristle teeth, stem densely covered with brown scales.** Fruit dots round. Occasional in woods at low and medium elevations.

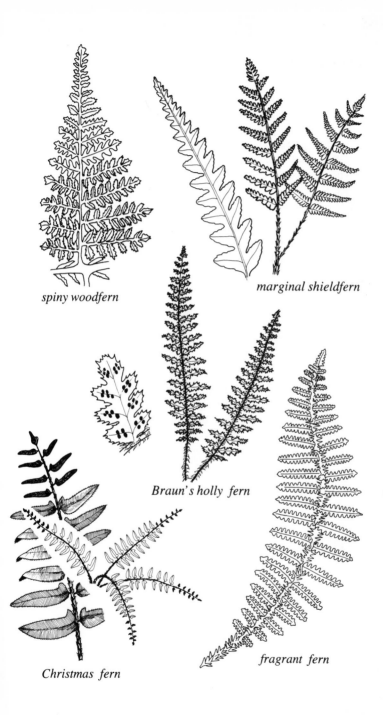

spiny woodfern

marginal shieldfern

Braun's holly fern

Christmas fern

fragrant fern

FERNS

FERN ALLIES

HORSETAIL   *Equisetum arvense*

Leaves small and scalelike, **stems prominent and grooved, often branching,** spore cases in a small cone. Common in wet areas mostly at low elevations. The stems are gritty due to the presence of silica, and have been used for scouring pots. There are several species that are distinguished by technical differences.

QUILLWORT   *Isoetes echinospora*

Small tufted grasslike plant with spore cases enclosed by the bases of the leaves. Occasional in shallow water or on wet shores of mountain ponds.

GRAPE FERN   *Botrychium dissectum*

Fernlike plant up to 1 foot high, blade horizontal and divided into many segments, **spore cases on a separate taller stalk.** Occasional in dry woods on lower slopes. Spores produced in the fall.

RATTLESNAKE FERN   *Botrychium virginianum*

Fernlike plant up to 2 feet high with horizontal blade finely divided into many segments, **spore-bearing stalk rising directly from the blade,** much larger than the preceding species. Occasional in hardwoods on lower slopes.

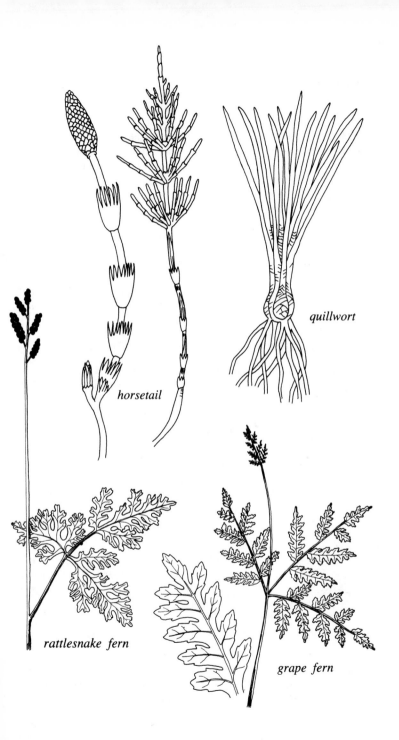

horsetail

quillwort

rattlesnake fern

grape fern

CLUBMOSSES

These plants are distinguished from the true mosses to which they are not related. They have woody stems and specialized cells that conduct water — which mosses lack — and are usually larger than mosses. In the age of dinosaurs they grew as large as trees. Some of the species have several common names. Only one or two names for each species are given here though other names could be considered equally correct. The spores are contained in spore cases located in terminal cones or at the base of the leaf.

Spore cases inconspicuous at the base of the leaves.

SHINING CLUBMOSS   *Lycopodium lucidulum*

Stem single or once-forked up to 1 foot high, **stem with belts of longer and shorter leaves.** Common on mountain slopes, especially in coniferous woods, occasional in the alpine zone.

FIR CLUBMOSS   *Lycopodium Selago*

Stems usually not more than 6 inches high, **tufted, leaves all about the same length.** Common on rocky summits and in the alpine zone, occasional on ledges at low elevations.

Spore cases in cones at the top of some of the stems.

BOG CLUBMOSS   *Lycopodium innundatum*

Sterile stems creeping, fertile stems up to 2 inches high with a **single cone with spore case scales resembling leaves.** Occasional in wet places at low elevations and in the alpine zone on Mansfield.

BRISTLY CLUBMOSS   *Lycopodium annotinum*

Main stem creeping on the surface of the ground, ascending branches forking and up to 1 foot high, **cones directly above the leaves.** Common in dry areas. In the alpine zone it is smaller and the leaves press close to the stem, resembling fir clubmoss.

STAGHORN CLUBMOSS   *Lycopodium clavatum*

Resembling bristly clubmoss but with **cones separated from leaves by stalks 1 inch or more long.** Common in dry woods on slopes, occasional under evergreens at high elevations. The soft branches suggest the young furry antlers of a deer.

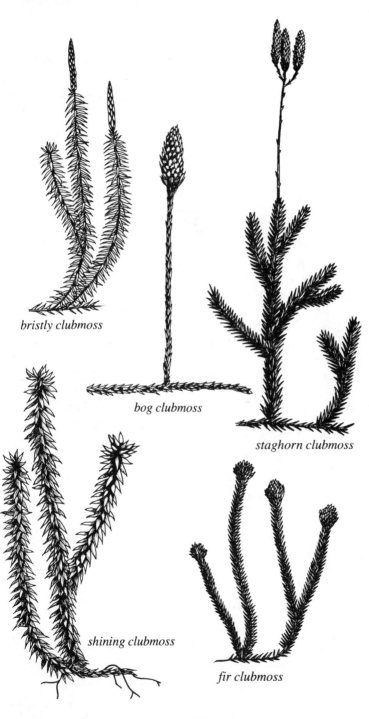

bristly clubmoss

bog clubmoss

staghorn clubmoss

shining clubmoss

fir clubmoss

GROUND CEDAR or RUNNING PINE
Lycopodium complanatum

Main stem creeping on surface of the ground, **branches and leaves flat** and fanlike, 1 to 4 cones at the end of a slender stalk. Common in dry woods on lower slopes, occasional under evergreens in the alpine zone.

ALASKA CLUBMOSS
Lycopodium sitchense

Somewhat resembling ground cedar, main stem creeping on the surface of the ground or just below it, **branchlets not flat, leaves small and pointed,** cones usually single on short stems or stemless. Rare in dry places on lower slopes and under evergreens in the alpine area.

GROUND PINE
Lycopodium obscurum

Main stem deep in the ground, **plants treelike up to 1 foot high with bushy forking branches,** several cones at the ends of the branches. Common in dry woods on lower slopes, occasionally ascending to higher elevations, in the alpine zone on Mansfield and Camel's Hump.

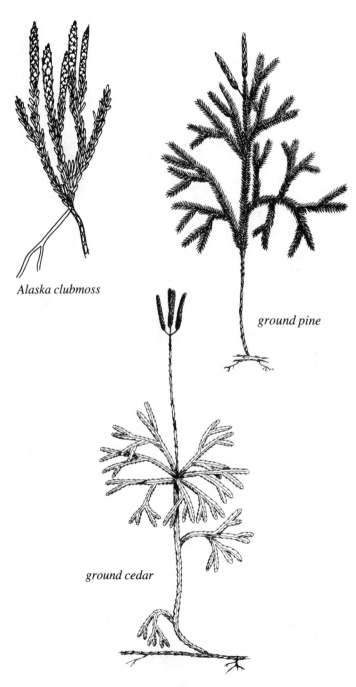

Alaska clubmoss

ground pine

ground cedar

Grasses
and
Grasslike Plants

As a group, the plants in this section can be recognized by their narrow grasslike leaves. All of the grasslike plants have flowers, with stamens that produce pollen and pistils that produce the seed. The flowers are small, inconspicuous, and dull green or brown. In the alpine area, much of what is often called grass is either alpine sedge or highland rush.

Organization

There are three families in this group — grass, rush, and sedge, the latter of which includes bulrushes and cotton grasses. Each family is described briefly at the head of its section.

Botanical Terms

The stems of grasses are round or nearly round. The leaves are two-ranked, that is, on opposite sides of the stem from each other. The sepals and petals of wildflowers are replaced by scales that are technically known as **glumes** and **lemmas**. The flowers (**florets**) are grouped in **spiklets**, each of which may contain one or several florets. The spikelets are usually grouped in **spikes**.

Awns, hairlike bristles, are often present on the florets. There are many species of grasses which are distinguished by technical differences. Only the alpine grasses and some of the easily recognized lowland ones are included in this guide.

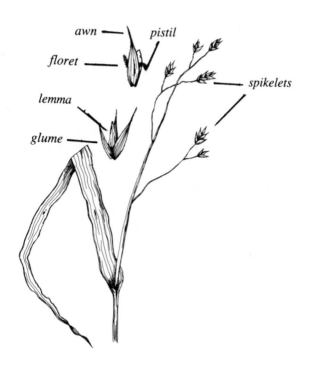

Entries

Each entry indicates height; distinguishing characteristics of stems, leaves, and flowers; and habitat and frequency.

GRASSES

GRASS FAMILY

FRINGED BROME   *Bromus ciliatus*

Tall grass up to 3 feet, spikelets with several florets, **spikelet branches drooping, resembling oats,** awns present. Occasional on open banks at low elevations, rare in grassy areas in alpine ravines.

FALSE MELIC   *Schizachne purpurascens*

Up to 3 feet high, spikelets with several florets in a thin narrow spike, **awns prominent and outcurving.** Frequent in dry woods and on lower slopes, rare in alpine ravines.

MOUNTAIN FESCUE   *Festuca prolifera*

Up to 1 foot high, narrow and curving spikelets with several florets, **some altered to leafy tufts.** Rare in alpine ravines on Washington and Katahdin.

MANNA GRASS   *Glyceria striata*

Up to 2 feet tall but often shorter, many small spikelets less than ¼ **inch long** with 5 to 9 small overlapping florets. Occasional in open wet areas and in alpine ravines. Other larger species of manna grass are more common at lower elevations.

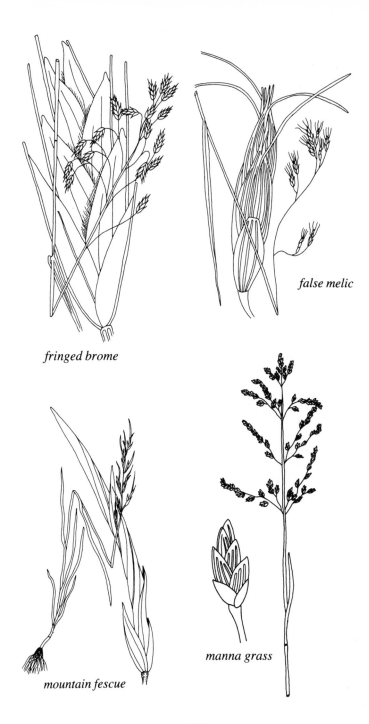

fringed brome

false melic

mountain fescue

manna grass

171

GRASSES

BLUEGRASS

Bluegrass is a common lowland grass of hayfields, distinguished by numerous small spikelets with a **sharp keel on the back** which can be seen on close examination.

ALPINE BLUEGRASS   *Poa alpigena*

New stems arising from **curving basal stems that rise out of old dried leaves.** Rare in wet places in alpine regions of Washington and Katahdin.

MOUNTAIN BLUEGRASS   *Poa glauca*

Low grass up to 1 foot high, leaves mostly at the base with 2 or 3 short ones on the stem. **Leaves and stem blue-green to whitish.** Frequent in open places in the alpine area, rare on cliffs at lower elevations.

WAVY BLUEGRASS   *Poa Fernaldiana*

Similar to the preceding but **stems very slender and often arching,** not blue-green. Frequent in open places in the alpine area, rare at lower elevations, mostly on ledges.

MOUNTAIN WITCHGRASS   *Agropyron trachycaulum*
or WHEATGRASS

Up to 2 feet high, spikelets forming **narrow spikes on opposite sides of the stem.** Resembles the common weedy lowland witchgrass but without elongate roots. Frequent on ledges and in rocky woods at low elevations, occasional in alpine ravines and alpine areas.

SPIKED TRISETUM   *Trisetum spicatum*

Somewhat similar to false melic but spikelets clustered in a rather thick spike, **awns prominent and recurving.** Occasional in alpine ravines and alpine areas.

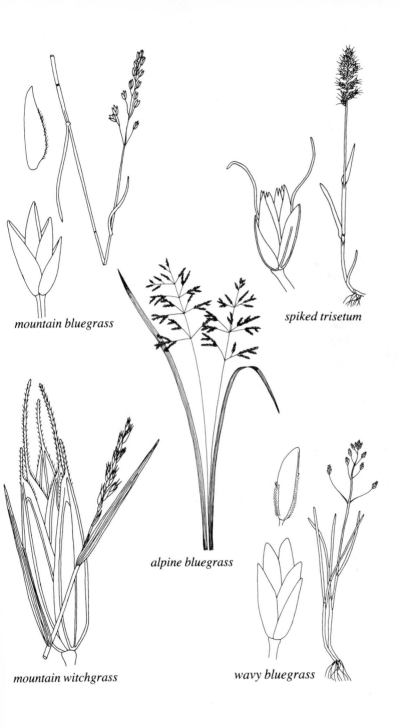

mountain bluegrass

spiked trisetum

alpine bluegrass

mountain witchgrass

wavy bluegrass

GRASSES

HAIRGRASS
Deschampsia flexuosa

Up to 2 feet tall, leaves mostly at the base of the stem, **thin and hairlike, forming soft tufts,** spikelets small. Frequent in dry woods and on ledges on the lower slopes, also in alpine ravines and alpine areas.

MOUNTAIN HAIRGRASS
Deschampsia atropurpurea

Somewhat lower than the preceding, leaves flat and soft, **spikelets on thin drooping stalks, awns small and bent,** sticking a short distance out of the floret. Frequent in the alpine areas of Washington and Katahdin, rare on Mansfield.

BLUEJOINT
or REED-BENTGRASS
Calamagrostis canadensis

Tall attractive grass up to 3 feet or more, spikelets small, one-flowered, **numerous and arranged in a branched plumelike cluster.** Common in wet places at low elevations, occasional in alpine ravines and in the alpine area. The alpine forms have larger spikelets than the lowland ones.

MOUNTAIN BLUEJOINT
Calamagrostis Pickeringii

Similar to the preceding but flower clusters narrower, **curving offshoot stems from the base of the main stem.** Occasional in moist alpine areas in the White Mountains, also at lower elevations in the Pemigewasset River valley.

NORTHERN BENTGRASS
Agrostis borealis

From 1 to 2 feet tall, **spikelets small in an open cluster.** Related and similar to the common redtop of hayfields and roadsides. Frequent in dry and rocky areas on the lower slopes, also in dry alpine areas where it is usually smaller than in the lowlands.

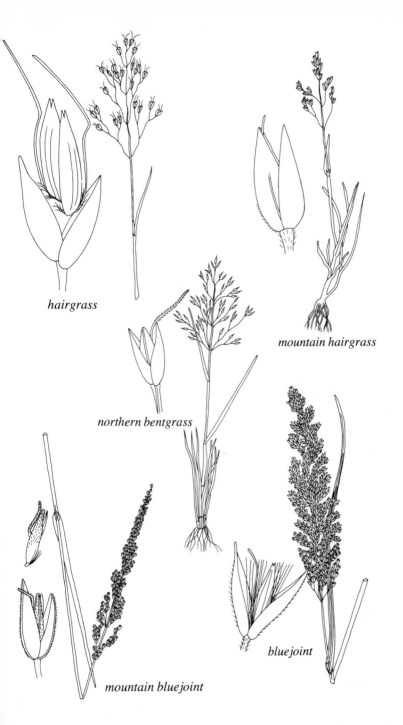

hairgrass

mountain hairgrass

northern bentgrass

bluejoint

mountain bluejoint

175

WOOD REEDGRASS
Cinna latifolia

Up to 3 feet high, **leaves up to ½ inch broad, 4 to 6 inches long,** spikelets small, one-flowered, in rather narrow clusters. Occasional in open woods and in alpine areas.

ALPINE TIMOTHY
Phleum alpinum

Up to 1 foot high, **spikelets in a dense thick spike less than 2 inches long.** Occasional in alpine regions of Katahdin and Washington. Resembles the common timothy of hayfields but smaller.

SHORTHUSK GRASS
Brachyelytrum erectum

Up to 3 feet high, leaves up to ½ inch wide, **short, up to 4 inches long,** spikelets narrow, **awns up to 4 inches long.** Frequent in dry woods at low elevations.

MILLET GRASS
Milium effusum

Up to 2 feet high, leaves up to ½ inch broad, spikelets with 1 floret and **tending to spread and separate.** Occasional in hardwoods at low elevations.

SWEETGRASS
Hierochloe odorata

Low, up to 1 foot high, **stem surrounded by dead leaves of previous year, stem leaves short, less than 1 inch long,** spikelets without awns. Occasional in dry areas at low elevations and in alpine ravines and alpine areas. The basal leaves are sweet-scented and have been used for Indian baskets.

ALPINE SWEETGRASS
Hierochloe alpina

Similar to the preceding, stem stiff, spikelets with **prominent awns ¼ inch long.** Frequent in alpine ravines and alpine areas.

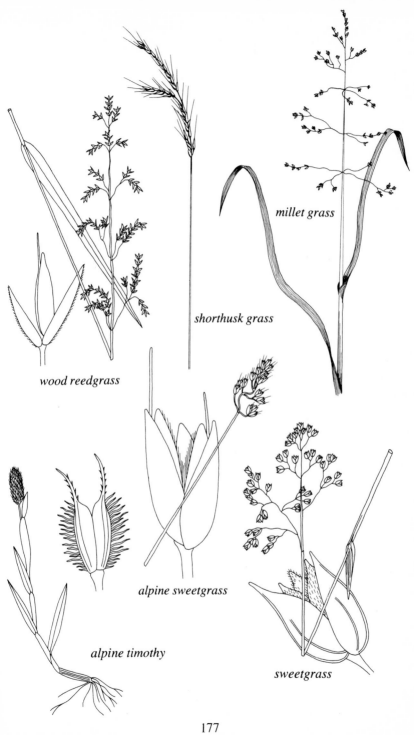

wood reedgrass

shorthusk grass

millet grass

alpine sweetgrass

alpine timothy

sweetgrass

177

SEDGE FAMILY

These plants resemble grasses but with important differences. The stems are usually triangular and the leaves are three-ranked; that is, three evenly-spaced leaves on one level on the stem. In the mountains there are 3 genera. **Bulrushes,** with one exception, are tall with a large cluster of spikes. **Cotton grass** has seeds surrounded by white bristles. The large genus **carex** has hard seeds, each enclosed in a papery pod, the pods grouped in spikes. Sedges are more common than grasses in the alpine region.

DEER'S HAIR   *Scirpus cespitosus*
or ALPINE BULRUSH

Usually less than 1 foot high, stem thin and wiry **without leaves, a single small spike at the top** less than ¼ inch long. Frequent in alpine regions in Maine, New Hampshire, and New York, rare on Mansfield (VT).

RED-BANDED SEDGE   *Scirpus rubrotinctus*

Tall, up to 3 feet high with **dark red bands on the stem**, a large cluster of many spikelets at the top. Frequent in open areas on lower slopes, rare near the tops of some mountains but not in alpine areas.

BLACK-BANDED SEDGE   *Scirpus atrocinctus*

Similar in appearance to the preceding, **a black band at the top of the stem.** Frequent in open wet areas at low elevations, occasional in alpine ravines.

HARE'S TAIL   *Eriophorum spissum*
or COTTON GRASS

1 to 3 feet high, no leaves on the stem, **single spike with a mass of white hairs,** resembles cotton. Frequent in peat bogs at all elevations. This is an easily recognized sedge.

CAPITATE SEDGE   *Carex capitata*

About 1 foot high, **stem without leaves and a single small spike at the top**, nearly round. Rare in dry areas on Washington and near the summit of Cardigan (NH).

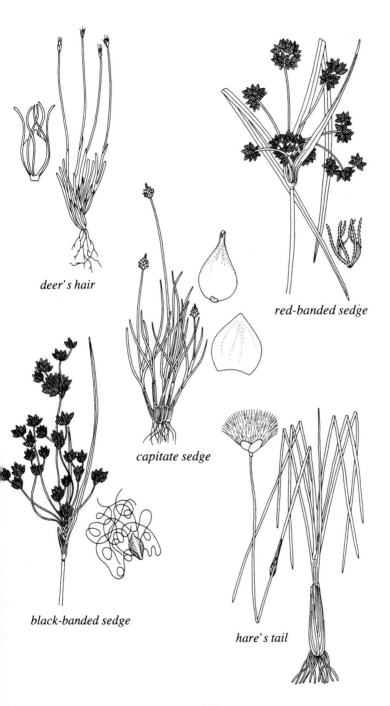

deer's hair

red-banded sedge

capitate sedge

black-banded sedge

hare's tail

179

GRASSES

THREE-SPIKED SEDGE
Carex trisperma

Leaves narrow, **stem thin and wiry, 2 or 3 small spikes.** Frequent in swamps and wet areas to high elevations but not in the alpine area.

SILVERY SEDGE
Carex canescens

1 to 2 feet tall, **stem and leaves with white bloom,** several spikes less than ½ inch long. Frequent in swamps and damp woods from low to high elevations, occasional in alpine ravines and alpine areas.

BROWN SEDGE
Carex brunnescens

About 1 foot high, similar to the preceding but without bloom, **spikes smaller**, less than ¼ inch long. Frequent on banks and in wet areas from low elevations to the alpine area.

MOUNTAIN SEDGE
Carex scirpoidea

Up to 1 foot high, leaves small and at the base of the stem, stamens and pistils on separate spikes, **each spike differing in appearance.** Occasional on wet rocks or wet turf mostly in alpine areas, but occasionally lower.

BRISTLE-LEAVED SEDGE
Carex eburnea

Up to 1 foot high, leaves **numerous, tufted, all at base of stem, thin and wiry,** spikes small, less than ¼ inch long. Rare on cliffs and in alpine areas in Vermont.

CUTLEAF SEDGE
Carex crinita

In clumps, 3 feet or more high, **spikes large and usually drooping, up to 3 inches long.** Common in wet areas at low elevations, occasional in alpine ravines. The leaves have sharp edges and can cause small cuts on your hands.

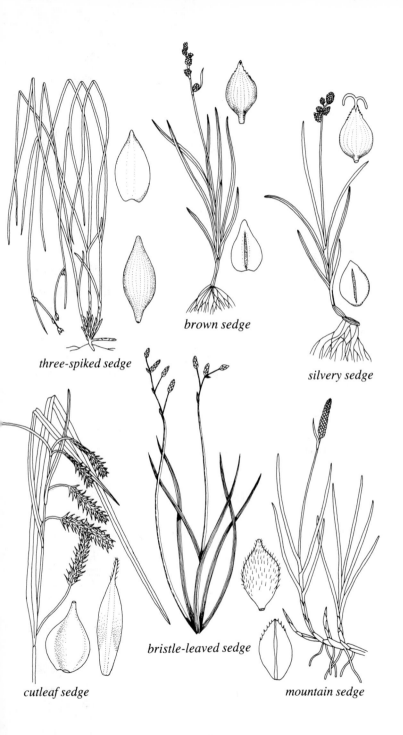

three-spiked sedge

brown sedge

silvery sedge

cutleaf sedge

bristle-leaved sedge

mountain sedge

GRASSES

ALPINE
or BIGELOW'S SEDGE
Carex Bigelowii

About 1 foot high, **most of the leafs in tufts at the base of the stem,** several narrow erect spikes about 1 inch long. Common in alpine areas, rare on lower peaks. This sedge forms alpine lawns.

TUSSOCK SEDGE
Carex lenticularis

3 feet or more high, **stems in dense clumbs or tussocks,** leaves narrow less than ⅛ inch broad, spikes up to 1 inch long, crowded and erect. Occasional in open wet places at low elevations and in alpine ravines.

BLACK SEDGE
Carex atratiformis

Resembles alpine sedge but **spikes shorter and thicker, about ¼ inch wide.** Rare in moist alpine areas of Washington and Katahdin.

MOUNTAIN BOG SEDGE
Carex paupercula

Up to 2 feet high, stems and leaves forming clumps, **scales on spikes with sharp tapering points.** Occasional in bogs and alpine ravines.

BOG SEDGE
Carex limosa

Resembles the preceding, up to 2 feet high, stems single, **scales on spikes without sharp points.** Occasional in bogs at low elevations.

FEW-FLOWERED SEDGE
Carex rariflora

Resembles the preceding but shorter and with **10 or fewer seed pods on spike.** Once found on Katahdin in a boggy area. Frequent in the arctic.

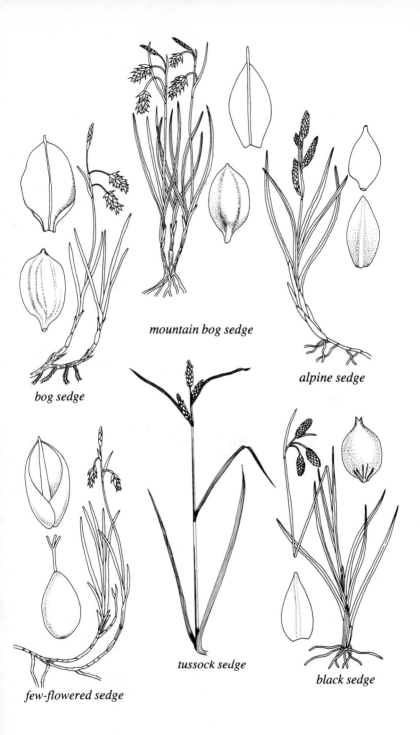

bog sedge

mountain bog sedge

alpine sedge

few-flowered sedge

tussock sedge

black sedge

DROOPING WOOD SEDGE   *Carex arctata*

Up to 3 feet high, base of stem purple, surrounded with dead leaves, **spikes thin and loosely flowered**, 1 to 2 inches long. Frequent in dry woods on the lower slopes.

HAIRLIKE SEDGE   *Carex capillaris*

Low, up to 8 inches high, in clumps, stems very thin, **spikes small, less than 1 inch long** on very thin stems. Rare in moist places in the alpine region of Washington.

INFLATED SEDGE   *Carex intumescens*

Up to 3 feet high, spikes nearly globular, **few florets with bladderlike inflated seed pods.** Frequent in dry woods at low and medium elevations.

BEAKED SEDGE   *Carex rostrata*

Up to 3 feet high, stem thick and spongy at base, **spikes large**, up to 3 inches long and ½ inch thick. Occasional at edges of ponds at low and medium elevations.

ROUND-SPIKED SEDGE   *Carex oligosperma*

Up to 3 feet high, leaves thin and nearly round in cross section, **1 or 2 globular spikes about 1 inch long.** Occasional in peat bogs at low and medium elevations.

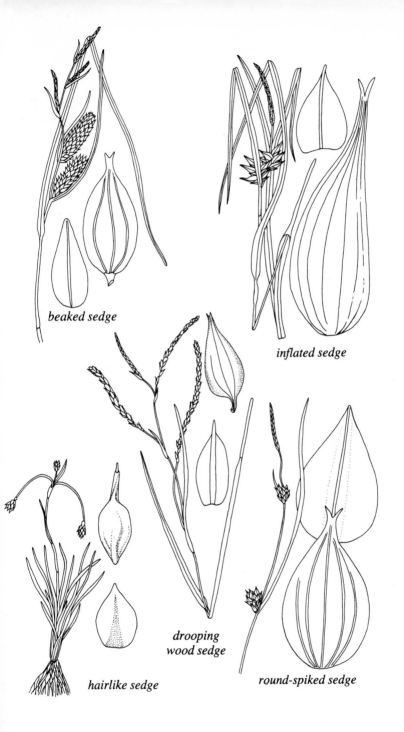

beaked sedge

inflated sedge

drooping wood sedge

hairlike sedge

round-spiked sedge

GRASSES

RUSH FAMILY

When not in fruit, these plants resemble grasses and sedges. The botanical distinction lies in the small brown sepals and petals of rushes, which in grasses and sedges are replaced by glumes and lemmas. The stems of rushes are usually round and in most species the leaves are at the base.

HIGHLAND RUSH   *Juncus trifidus*

6 inches to 2 feet high, stems stiff surrounded at bottom with stiff spikes of old leaf bases, **2 or 3 thin leaves at summit surrounding small spikes.** Common in dry alpine areas, also on bare summits of some of the lower mountains, occasional on dry cliffs at lower elevations. Next to alpine sedge this is the most common grasslike plant in the alpine zone.

THREAD RUSH   *Juncus filiformis*

6 inches to 2 feet high, stem leafless with a few short leaves at the base, **small flower or seed clusters about ⅔ of the way up the stem.** Frequent in boggy or wet areas at low elevations, occasional in boggy places in the alpine zone.

SHORT-TAILED RUSH   *Juncus brevicaudatus*

1 to 2 feet high, leaves narrow and mostly near the base, **flowers or seed pods in small 3 to 7 flowered heads.** Frequent in wet places at low elevations, occasional in alpine ravines.

SMALL-FLOWERED WOODRUSH   *Luzula parviflora*

1 to 2 feet high, basal leaves ½ inch broad, **flowers or seed pods loosely spreading on thin stems.** Frequent in damp woods at low elevations, occasional in alpine ravines and alpine area.

ALPINE WOODRUSH   *Luzula spicata*

6 to 15 inches high, numerous narrow leaves at the base of the stem, 2 or 3 partway up the stem, **flowers crowded in nodding or drooping spikes ½ to 1½ inches long.** Common in alpine lawns on Washington, also on Katahdin and in the Adirondacks.

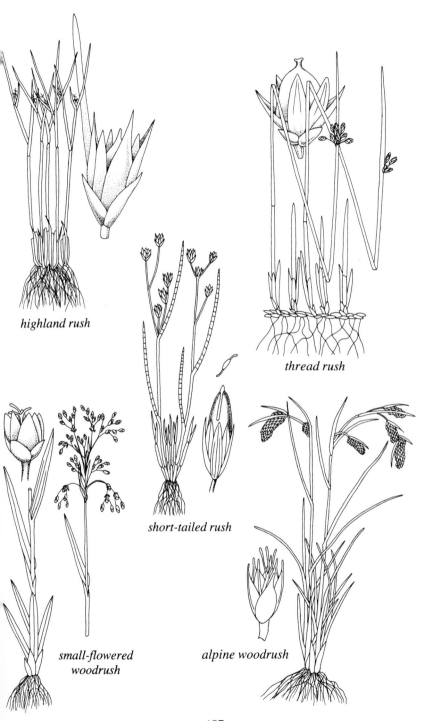

highland rush

thread rush

short-tailed rush

small-flowered
woodrush

alpine woodrush

ARCTIC WOODRUSH · *Luzula confusa*

Similar to the preceding, **flower clusters in globular spikes ¼ inch in diameter** on thin stems. Rare on Washington and Katahdin, more common in the arctic.

MANY-FLOWERED WOODRUSH · *Luzula multiflora*

1 to 2 feet high, often in clumps, numerous leaves at the base, few on the stem, **flowering spikes egg-shaped, small, less than ½ inch long** on thin stems. Occasional in grassy areas at low and medium elevations.

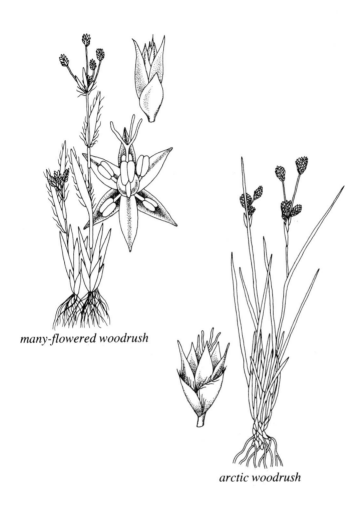

many-flowered woodrush

arctic woodrush

Birds

This field guide focuses on birds that can be found along mountain trails. While intended to provide a complete list of those birds that breed on slopes and mountaintops in spring and summer, it also includes some fall and winter migrants, as well as lowland birds found in open land near the foot of the trail. Serious birders will wish to supplement this guide with any of several excellent bird guides that are available.

Organization

In all instances but the first — a diverse group of birds found near ponds and marshes — the birds in this guide are classified by families, such as the woodpecker, thrush, and warbler families. As an aid to identification, some families similar in appearance (such as swallows and swifts) or behavior (nuthatches and creepers) are further grouped together.

Entries

Each entry covers the important characteristics you will need to note to identify a bird — size, coloration, song and call — as well as the bird's habits and habitat (including elevation), frequency of appearance, and seasonal migration.

Size is helpful in identifying birds, but it is not always easy to judge. The well-known sparrow, robin, and crow are used here as standards of size comparison. More reliable field marks than size are a bird's coloration and special markings such as wing bars, eye stripe, streaked or spotted breast, and tail bands. You will observe that in some families such as the warbler and grosbeak the males are distinctively colored while the females and immature birds lack vivid color and markings.

When you become familiar with various birds of the mountainsides, you may find that they are most accurately identified by their songs. The ability to identify birds by their songs does not happen overnight, however; it requires much careful listening and time in the field. Though bird songs are difficult to describe, an attempt has been made here.

The usefulness of noting a bird's habits and habitat should not be underestimated. Some birds are usually found on the ground, while others are excellent fliers and spend most of the time in the air. Similarly, you can expect to find some birds on the trunk or branch of a tree searching for insects, or flitting in a treetop, or near water. The elevation range provided in each entry is helpful in confirming identification, as are the lists of birds common to low and high elevations and the alpine area found at the end of this introduction.

Birds are most easily observed and identified from May to July. At that time they are in their breeding plumage and sing vociferously. You will enjoy listening to bird song even if you cannot identify the singer.

Birds common at both low and high elevations

Nashville warbler
myrtle warbler
white-throated sparrow
slate-colored junco
spruce grouse
ruby-crowned kinglet
golden-crowned kinglet
Swainson's thrush
purple finch
pine siskin
raven

Birds common at high elevations and in the alpine area

blackpoll warbler
gray-cheeked thrush
boreal chickadee
yellow-bellied flycatcher
pipit (Katahdin)

ACCIPITER HAWKS

Accipiters have long tails and short rounded wings. They do not soar but alternately flap and sail, and are usually confined to woodlands. Accipiters feed on small mammals and birds.

COOPER'S HAWK — *Accipiter cooperii*

Length 15 inches, smaller than a crow. Adults have rusty, barred breasts, bluish backs, and rounded tails. Immature birds have streaked breasts and brown backs. Call a series of cackling notes. Summer resident, occasional in open woodlands and wood margins.

SHARP-SHINNED HAWK — *Accipiter striatus*

Resembles Cooper's hawk but smaller, 10 to 14 inches, tail narrower and more square-cut. Summer resident, frequent in woodlands but a rapid flier and not often seen. Near a chicken farm this bird can be destructive; in the woods it helps maintain the natural balance of bird populations. Not illustrated.

GOSHAWK — *Accipiter gentilis*

Resembles the sharp-shinned hawk but larger. Length 20 inches, larger than a crow, white stripe over the eye. Call a series of high notes. Summer resident, occasional in woods on mountain slopes. It becomes quite aggressive when its nest is approached.

BUTEO HAWKS

Buteos are somewhat larger than accipiters and have broad rounded tails. They soar high in the air and are occasionally seen flying over mountains. They feed mostly on mice.

BROAD-WINGED HAWK — *Buteo platypterus*

Length 13 inches, wing span 33 inches, prominent dark and white bands on tail. Call a thin, shrill whistle. Common in lowlands.

RED-TAILED HAWK — *Buteo jamaicensis*

Length 18 inches, wing span 48 inches. Resembles the broad-winged hawk but without bands on its tail. Upper side of tail rufous-red, which can be seen as the bird turns. Call a faint, high, descending scream. Common summer resident in lowlands.

Cooper's hawk

goshawk

broad-winged hawk

red-tailed hawk

193

BIRDS

WATER BIRDS

Because this is an alpine guide, the number of pond and marsh birds you will see is limited. Therefore, water and marsh birds of many families are grouped together here under one heading.

BLACK DUCK   *Anas rubripes*

A surface-feeding duck 16 inches long, mostly black with white wing linings that are prominent in flight. Call 2 or 3 loud "quacks." Summer resident, occasional in ponds at lower elevations. In looking for ducks, approach a pond quietly. Ducks are easily frightened and take off in rapid, low flight.

GREAT BLUE HERON   *Ardea herodias*

Stands about 4 feet tall with long yellow bill, long neck, and long legs, coloration bluish-gray. In flight, neck is folded and legs dangle behind. Call a hoarse croak. Summer resident, occasional in ponds on lower slopes. When fishing, the heron wades slowly or stands motionless, waiting for a chance to spear a polywog or small fish.

BITTERN   *Botaurus lentignosus*

Stands about 30 inches tall, usually motionless, and with its bill pointed straight up. Mostly brown with a black mark on its neck. Call a low, repeated "onk-a-chonk" that from a distance has the sound of pounding in a stake. Summer resident, occasional in marshes and on edges of ponds on the lower slopes. The bird is well camouflaged and most likely to be noticed by its call.

SPOTTED SANDPIPER   *Actitis macularia*

Seven inches long with a long thin bill. Bobs continually up and down. Flies with a short wing stroke, with wings below the horizontal. Call a shrill "peet-weet." Summer resident, frequent on muddy edges of ponds and streams at low elevations. The sandpiper is most often seen running along muddy or sandy shores and is quite well camouflaged. When it flies, it stays close to the ground or water.

black duck

bittern

great blue heron

spotted sandpiper

195

WOODCOCK
Philohela minor

Brown, 8 inches long with a long bill. Call a nasal "peent" repeated at intervals. Summer resident, frequent in wet places at low elevations, especially in alder swamps. The woodcock is largely nocturnal and most likely to be heard at dusk in the spring. After a number of "peents" it may fly high in the air giving off a rapid twittering. It is not likely to be noticed in the summer unless you get close enough to flush it.

BELTED KINGFISHER
Megaceryle alcyon

Length 12 inches, grayish-blue and white, with a prominent bill and rather large head. Call a loud harsh rattle. Summer resident, frequent along larger streams and ponds at low elevations. The kingfisher is likely to be seen perched on the branch of a tree near a stream. If it sees a fish, it dives headfirst to catch it.

GROUSE

Grouse are large, plump, ground dwellers, a relative of the turkey, pheasant, and quail.

RUFFED GROUSE or PARTRIDGE
Bonasa umbellus

Length 14 inches, brown with bands on its tail. Permanent resident, common in woods and bushy areas. Call a soft drumming of the wings that starts slowly and becomes more rapid. The partridge, when approached, flies off suddenly with a noisy "whir." During the nesting season, the female attempts to lead an intruder away from her young by squealing and running along the ground feigning a broken wing. Care should be taken not to step on young birds, which are well camouflaged.

SPRUCE GROUSE
Canachites canadensis

Resembles ruffed grouse but darker. Male has dark tail with chestnut band at tip, red above the eye. Female's brown terminal band more noticeable, not spotted. Usually silent but occasionally gives a low-pitched hoot. Permanent resident, rare in coniferous forest on mountain slopes. The spruce grouse is tame and easily approached. Formerly the easy prey of hunters carrying sticks, it is now protected.

woodcock

belted kingfisher

ruffed grouse

spruce grouse

197

BIRDS

OWLS

Largely nocturnal, owls are birds of prey with large heads, short necks, and large eyes set in facial disks. Their flight is quiet and mothlike. They eat a variety of small mammals and some birds, disgorging the indigestible parts in the form of pellets.

GREAT HORNED OWL   *Bubo virginianus*

Length 20 inches, eyes yellow, prominent ear tufts, horizontal bars on breast. Call "hoo, hoo" repeated 4 to 6 times with about the same rhythm and inflection. Permanent resident, occasional in woods on mountain slopes. This is the largest and most powerful of the owls. It has been known to attack man when its nest was approached.

BARRED OWL   *Strix minor*

Length 17 inches, resembles the great horned owl but no ear tufts and eyes brown. Call "hoo, hoo, hoo, h', hoooo" with a break in the rhythm and often ending in a descending drawn-out "hooaw." Permanent resident, frequent in deep woodlands or wooded swamps. This is the most common owl in the mountains and is most likely to be noticed by its call. It occasionally emits harsh screams, whines, and other sounds as well.

SAW-WHET OWL   *Aegolius acadicus*

A small owl, length 7 inches, with no ear tufts. Call a low whistled note that may be repeated 100 times, at other times a sound resembling the filing of a saw. Permanent resident, occasional in forests or wooded swamps at low elevations. This bird may be seen roosting in a tree, but it is more likely to be noticed by its call.

HUMMINGBIRDS

Hummingbirds are the smallest of North American birds and only one species is found in the East.

RUBY-THROATED HUMMINGBIRD   *Archilochus colubris*

Length 3 inches, bill slender, rapid wingbeats that produce a humming sound. Call occasional shrill chirps or squeaks. Summer resident, occasional on lower slopes of mountains in open areas near ponds. Hummingbirds feed on nectar in flowers while hovering. Expert fliers, they can fly backward and have no enemies because no other bird can catch them.

great horned owl

barred owl

saw-whet owl

ruby-throated hummingbird

WOODPECKERS

Woodpeckers have strong bills for drilling. They cling to the trunks of trees in a vertical position and hammer holes in the wood, nesting in holes they have carved out of dead trees. The woodpecker's flight is undulating, a series of flaps alternated with coasting, wings held close to the body while gliding.

HAIRY WOODPECKER *Dendrocopus villosus*

Length 9 to 10 inches, white streak on back, bill ¾ as long as head, male with a small red patch on its head. Call a loud "peek," also a rattle. Permanent resident, common in woods on mountain slopes.

DOWNY WOODPECKER *Dendrocopus pubescens*

Length 7½ inches, bill less than half the length of the head. Resembles the hairy woodpecker but smaller, and with bill much shorter in proportion to the head. Call similar to the hairy's. Permanent resident, common in woods on mountain slopes. After both woodpeckers have been seen several times it is not difficult to distinguish between the two. Both feed on a variety of insects found in the bark of trees.

PILEATED WOODPECKER *Dryocopus pileatus*

Length 15 inches, black back, red crest on head. In flight looks like a crow but with prominent white markings. Call a loud "kuk, kuk, kuk." Permanent resident, occasional in woods on mountain slopes where the trees are large. This woodpecker is specialized in its diet, eating only carpenter ants and a few other large insects. It is shy and infrequently seen. Holes 1-3 inches across in a partly dead tree, with chips on the ground, are visible evidence of the work of a pileated woodpecker.

BLACK-BACKED THREE-TOED WOODPECKER *Picoides arcticus*

Length 8 inches, back solid black, male has a yellow cap. Call a sharp "chirk." Permanent resident, rare in forests on mountain slopes. This woodpecker taps softly and flakes off the bark rather than drilling into it. It is specialized in its diet and prefers bark insects that occur in trees that have been dead for a year or two. Its work can often be recognized, especially on spruce trees, by reddish spots where the outer bark has been removed.

hairy woodpecker

downy woodpecker

pileated woodpecker

black-backed three-toed woodpecker

BIRDS

NORTHERN THREE-TOED WOODPECKER
Picoides tridactylus

Length 7 inches, back with horizontal black and white stripes, male has a yellow cap. Formerly known as "ladder-back" because of the markings on its back, which resembles the sapsucker's though the markings on the head are distinctly different. Call a "chirk." Permanent resident, rare in forests on mountain slopes. In habit it resembles the black-backed, but occurs in much smaller numbers and is seldom seen.

YELLOW-BELLIED SAPSUCKER
Sphyrapicus varius

Length 8 inches, prominent long white wing strips. Call a squealing "whoee" slurring downward. Summer resident, frequent in deciduous or mixed woods on mountain slopes. The sapsucker taps softly when hunting for food. Its mating tapping is louder, starting off rapidly and ending slowly. In addition to sap, it eats inner bark; a horizontal row of holes on the trunk of a tree, the result of its work, can often be seen, especially on mountain ash.

FLICKER
Colaptes auratus

Length 11 inches, brown back, prominent white patch on rump visible in flight. Call a series of "kuk, kuk, kuk" resembling the pileated woodpecker but not as loud. Summer resident, common in open country in the lowlands, occasional in woods on lower slopes. The flicker is a woodpecker that spends most of its time on the ground hunting for ants and other insects. As do other woodpeckers, it excavates a hole in a tree for its nest.

FLYCATCHERS

Flycatchers perch on branches waiting to swoop forth in pursuit of insects. They are short-billed grayish birds whose songs are distinctive.

PHOEBE
Sayornis phoebe

Length 6 inches, dark head, no wing bars, wags its tail at frequent intervals. Song a short distinct "fee-be," not whistled like that of the chickadee. Summer resident, common in open areas in the lowlands, especially near buildings, and occasionally ascending to alpine zones.

northern three-toed woodpecker

yellow-bellied sapsucker

flicker

phoebe

203

BIRDS

WOOD PEWEE

Contopus virens

Length 5 inches, 2 white wing bars. Song a plaintive, drawn-out, whistled "pee-a-wee." Summer resident, common in woods on mountain slopes at low elevations. The pewee is a nondescript bird, not often seen, but the song is distinctive.

OLIVE-SIDED FLYCATCHER

Nuttallornis borealis

Length 7 inches, resembles the wood pewee but with white throat and dark patches on the sides of its chest. Song a melodious whistle, "whit-three-beers," with a distinctive rhythm. Common in coniferous or mixed woods on mountain slopes to medium elevations. It often perches on the top of a dead tree or on an exposed branch, from which it makes sallies in pursuit of insects.

LEAST FLYCATCHER
or CHEBEC

Empidonax minimus

Small flycatcher, length 4½ inches, with 2 white wing bars. Song a short "che-bek" repeated at frequent intervals. Summer resident, common in lowlands and occasional in open and wooded areas on mountain slopes at low elevations. This bird is tame and easily approached. It is best recognized by its song.

YELLOW-BELLIED FLYCATCHER

Empidonax flaviventris

Length 4½ inches, resembles least flycatcher but has a yellow throat. Song a whistled "per-wee" or a short "killic." Summer resident, frequent in woods from medium to high elevations. This bird is common to mountaintops and subalpine zones. It is easily identified by its call, because in its habitat there is no other flycatcher to confuse it with.

wood pewee

olive-sided flycatcher

least flycatcher

yellow-bellied flycatcher

BIRDS

SWALLOWS AND SWIFTS

Swallows and swifts are often found together. They spend much of the time in the air, darting and turning in pursuit of insects. Both are excellent flyers.

BARN SWALLOW   *Hirundo rustica*

Length 6 inches, blue above, rusty beneath, forked tail. Song a twittering series of "wit, wit." Summer resident, frequent in open areas and on ponds on lower slopes. Occasionally flies over ridges and mountaintops. The barn swallow is most likely to be seen over a pond pursuing insects. Look for the forked tail.

TREE SWALLOW   *Iridoprocne bicolor*

Length 5 inches, blue or green above, white beneath. Song similar to the barn swallow's. Frequent in open areas on lower slopes and over ponds. Occasionally flies over ridges and mountaintops. It is most readily distinguished from the barn swallow by its tail, which is notched but not deeply forked.

CHIMNEY SWIFT   *Chaetura pelagiea*

Nearly black, cigar-shaped body, an excellent flier. Resembles a swallow, but appears to beat its wings alternately. Call a series of rapid short chirps. Summer resident, infrequent in the mountains in open areas at low elevations.

JAYS, CROWS AND RAVENS

Jays and crows are medium to large omniverous birds with heavy bills. Ravens, which resemble but are larger than crows, tend to be carrion feeders.

BLUE JAY   *Cyanocitta cristata*

Length 10 inches, prominent blue and white markings. Call most often a harsh "jeah," also various other calls, some clear and musical. Permanent resident, common in open areas and hardwoods on lower slopes. The blue jay can be recognized in flight as a bird larger than a robin with a flash of blue and white.

barn swallow

tree swallow

chimney swift

blue jay

207

BIRDS

GRAY
or CANADA JAY

Perisoreus canadensis

Length 10 inches, same size as blue jay, gray back, black cap on head. Call a rather soft "whee-oo," also various other notes. Permanent resident, rare in coniferous woods and lumbered areas up to high elevations. The gray jay was formerly common near lumber camps but is now rarely seen. It is quite tame.

CROW

Corvus brachyrhynchos

Length 17 inches, all black. Call a harsh distinctive "caw." Summer resident with some wintering in the lowlands, infrequent in the mountains, but may be seen in the air from mountaintops. It is distinguished from a hawk by the steady flapping of its wings, with only occasional gliding. In alpine areas it may be confused with the raven.

RAVEN

Corvus corax

Length 21 inches, resembles a crow but larger. Call a croaking "cruk." Permanent resident, frequent in the mountains near cliffs and in alpine areas. Although larger than a crow this is not a good field mark. It soars rather than flaps, and sometimes tumbles. Its voice too is different. The raven was formerly rare but in recent years has become much more common.

CHICKADEES

Chickadees are small birds with small stubby bills. They actively work along branches, often hanging upside down, searching for insects. They are unafraid of people and easily approached.

BLACK-CAPPED CHICKADEE

Parus atricapillus

Length 4½ inches, black cap and throat. Call a rather distinct "chick-a-dee-dee" and in the breeding season a song: a clear whistled "fee-be," easily imitated. Permanent resident, common on mountain slopes at low and medium elevations, occasional at high elevations. This is the most common bird along the trail. It is quite tame and easily attracted by making a squeaking sound.

gray jay

crow

raven

black-capped chickadee

209

BOREAL
or BROWN-CAPPED CHICKADEE
Parus hudsonicus

Resembles the black-capped chickadee but top of head is brown. Call a "chick-a-dee" but hoarse and nasal, no whistled song. Permanent resident, common in coniferous woods on the upper slopes and in the subalpine zone, occasional at low elevations. This is a bird to look for as you approach the top of a mountain. It is not difficult to get near enough to see the brown cap and, with a little practice, it is readily identified by its nasal call notes.

NUTHATCHES AND CREEPERS

Nuthatches and creepers are small birds that spend their time on the trunks of trees searching for insects. Creepers brace themselves with their tails, nuthatches do not.

WHITE-BREASTED NUTHATCH
Sitta carolinensis

Length 5 inches, breast white. Call a nasal rather loud "yank, yank," in the spring a series of "whys" all on the same pitch. Permanent resident, common in hardwoods on the lower slopes of mountains. This bird has a thin bill with which it probes bark for insects. It often goes down the tree upside down, head toward the ground.

RED-BREASTED NUTHATCH
Sitta canadensis

Resembles the white-breasted nuthatch but smaller, length 4 inches, breast reddish, white stripe through the eye. Call a "yank, yank," more nasal and softer than the white-breasted's. Permanent resident, common at low and medium elevations. This bird wanders around the trunk of a tree, often sideways, but only occasionally upside down.

BROWN CREEPER
Certhia familiaris

Length 4½ inches, brown back, curved bill. Call a single high thin "see;" song, heard in early spring, is a series of high thin notes. Permanent resident, frequent in forests on mountain slopes at low and medium elevations. It is well camouflaged against the trunk of a tree, where it can be found working its way slowly upward in search of insects. If you hear a thin high note, look carefully on tree trunks for the brown creeper.

red-breasted nuthatch

boreal chickadee

brown creeper

white-breasted nuthatch

211

BIRDS

THRUSHES

Thrushes are a family of fine singers. Most of them are brown and spend much of the time on the ground searching for worms, insects, and fruit. Included in this family is the robin, whose young have speckled breasts and are thrushlike in appearance.

HERMIT THRUSH   *Hylocichla guttata*

Length 6 inches, spotted breast, brown back, reddish tail. Song varied, flutelike phrases in a series of 3 to 6, tending to become increasingly higher in pitch. Summer resident, frequent in woods at low and medium elevations. Many people consider its song to be the best of any New Hampshire bird. It is heard occasionally during the day, but more often in the late afternoon or evening.

WOOD THRUSH   *Hylocichla mustelina*

Length 7 inches, rusty head, brown back, numerous large dark spots on breast. Song of separate phrases resembling the hermit thrush's, but each phrase followed by a guttural trill. Summer resident, frequent in woods on the lower slopes. The song is most often heard in the late afternoon or evening.

VEERY   *Hylocichla fuscesens*

Length 6 inches, rusty back, spots on breast indistinct or almost lacking. Song a whistled flute like series of "vee-a, vee-a" each successive one lower in pitch. Summer resident, frequent in deciduous woods on lower slopes. Song is usually heard in late afternoon and continues through twilight.

SWAINSON'S   *Hylocichla ustulata*
or OLIVE-BACKED THRUSH

Length 6 inches, olive-brown back, buffy face, and distinct eye ring. Song a series of flutelike phrases resembling the veery's but ascending the scale. Summer resident, frequent on mountain slopes from low to high elevations. This thrush is much more common in the mountains than in the lowlands.

hermit thrush

wood thrush

veery

Swainson's thrush

213

GRAY-CHEEKED THRUSH *Hylocichla minima*

Length 6 inches. Resembles the Swainson's thrush but eye ring inconspicuous. Song somewhat like the veery's but thinner and more nasal, often rising at the end. Summer resident, frequent near the tops of mountains, in ravines, and at the edge of the alpine zone. Look for this bird as you approach the top of a mountain. It is not often seen, but its song is distinctive.

ROBIN *Turdus migratorius*

Length 8 inches, orange breast. Song a series of whistled phrases of 2 or 3 notes each. Summer resident, common in open areas in lowlands and at the foot of mountains, occasionally seen in the alpine areas, especially in fall. This bird is familiar to all. In judging the size of an unfamiliar bird, it is often helpful to compare it to a robin's.

WRENS AND PIPITS

Wrens and pipits are slender-billed birds that hold their tails in distinctive poses: the wren's cocked upward, and the pipit's wagging continually. Both spend much of the time on the ground or in low bushes.

WINTER WREN *Troglodytes troglodytes*

Length 3½ inches, brown, tail short and stubby, cocked upward. Song a rapid musical succession of high warbles and trills lasting about 5 seconds. Summer resident, frequent in woods on mountain slopes at low and medium elevations. The winter wren can be found on the ground, bobbing through brush piles, mossy tangles, and roots. Its song is distinctive and easily recognized.

AMERICAN PIPIT *Anthus spinoletta*

Length 5½ inches, mostly brown, outer tail feathers white, bobs its tail. Call "pipit." Occasional in alpine areas during migration, breeds on Katahdin.

gray-cheeked thrush

robin

winter wren

American pipit

215

BIRDS

KINGLETS

Kinglets are small, active, thin-billed birds that flit around trees hunting for insects.

GOLDEN-CROWNED KINGLET *Regulus satrapa*

Length 3½ inches, yellow cap, white eye stripe, white wing bars. Song a series of thin high notes rising up the scale and then dropping. Call a thin high "zee." Permanent resident, frequent in coniferous woods from low to high elevations. The kinglet is so active it is hard to get a good look at it. Its call and small size help to identify it.

RUBY-CROWNED KINGLET *Regulus calendula*

Length 3½ inches. 2 white wing bars, ruby crown not always conspicuous. Song rather long, starting with high thin "zee, zee," skipping triplets in the middle then becoming weak. Summer resident, frequent in evergreen woods, especially boggy ones, from low to high elevations. The long bubbling song is distinctive. The winter wren also has a long song, though quite different.

VIREOS

Vireos are plain-colored, slow-moving birds that spend most of their time in the tops of trees looking for insects.

RED-EYED VIREO *Vireo olivaceous*

Length 5 inches, olive-green back, white stripe through red eye, no wing bars. Song a series of robinlike phrases with pauses between, repeated many times. Summer resident, common in deciduous and mixed forests at low to medium elevations. This vireo sings incessantly throughout the day.

golden-crowned kinglet

ruby-crowned kinglet

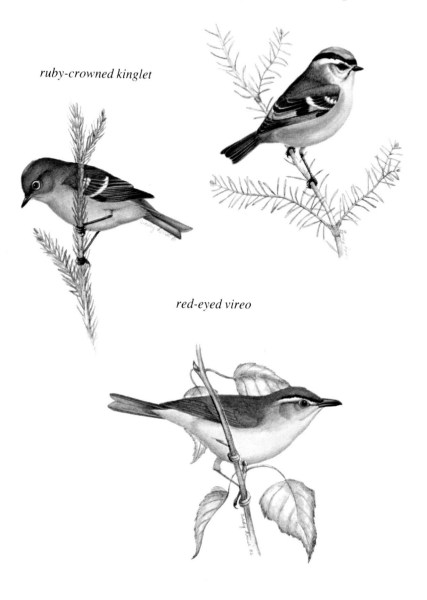

red-eyed vireo

SOLITARY *Vireo solitarius*
or BLUE-HEADED VIREO

Length 5 inches. Resembles the red-eyed vireo but with white wing bars, white eye ring, and white throat. Song similar to the red-eyed vireo's, but with more varied phrases and not repeated as many times per minute. Summer resident, frequent in deciduous and mixed woods at low to medium elevations. In summer this bird is less likely to be heard than the red-eyed vireo.

PHILADELPHIA VIREO *Vireo philadelphicus*

Length 5 inches, resembles red-eyed vireo but breast yellowish. Song closely resembles the red-eyed vireo's but slower and higher in pitch. Summer resident, infrequent in open bushy areas at low and medium elevations, tending to be found higher on the slopes than the other vireos, especially in areas where the heart-leaved white birch has replaced the lowland white birch. The habitat may help to distinguish it from the other vireos.

FINCHES, GROSBEAKS AND SPARROWS

Finches, grosbeaks, and sparrows comprise a large family of birds. They are seed-eaters and have short conical bills well adapted for cracking seeds.

PURPLE FINCH *Carpodacus purpureus*

Length 5½ inches, brown back, rosy red breast. Song a long melodious warble. Permanent resident, frequent in open woods from low to high elevations. The purple finch is the state bird of New Hampshire. Some remain all winter, but many migrate up from the south in spring.

GOLDFINCH *Spinus tristis*

Length 4½ inches, yellow with black and white wings. Song long, high, and clear, call "per-chic-o-ree." Permanent resident, frequent in bushy areas and open woods at low elevations. The goldfinch is common in the lowlands in summer, some remain during the winter.

Philadelphia vireo

solitary vireo

purple finch

goldfinch

PINE SISKIN
Spinus pinus

Length 4½ inches, brown with some yellow on wings and tail. Call a wheezy "shree." Winter visitor to coniferous woods on mountain slopes, irregularly frequent in summer.

RED CROSSBILL
Loxia curvirostra

Length 5½ inches, brick-red with darker wings. Call "kip, kip." Winter visitor to coniferous woods on mountain slopes, occasional in summer.

WHITE-WINGED CROSSBILL
Loxia leucoptera

Length 6 inches, red with black and white wings. Song a loud warble and trill, call a "peet." Winter visitor to coniferous woods on mountain slopes, occasional in summer.

SLATE-COLORED JUNCO
Junco hyemalis

Length 5½ inches, gray with white underparts and white outer tail feathers, which are prominent in flight. Song a muscial trill, all notes on the same pitch. Summer resident, common in open woods and bushy areas at all elevations, including alpine zones. A common and characteristic bird song of ravines and alpine areas is that of the junco. It may be found nesting in a crevice in rocks above treeline.

pine siskin

red crossbill

white-winged
crossbill

slate-colored junco

WHITE-THROATED SPARROW   *Zonotrichia albicollis*

Length 6 inches, prominent white throat, white eye stripe. Song a clear whistle easily imitated, "Old Sam Peabody, Peabody." Summer resident, common in undergrowth and bushes at all elevations. The song, which carries a long distance, is the easiest bird song to recognize in the alpine area.

SONG SPARROW   *Melospiza melodia*

Length 5½ inches, heavily streaked breast with a central dark spot. Song a varied series of trills and chirps. Summer resident, frequent in open and bushy areas on the lower slopes. The song sparrow is a common lowland bird, tending to be tame. It may be found near the foot of the trail.

LINCOLN'S SPARROW   *Melospiza Lincolnii*

Length 5½ inches, resembles song sparrow but breast streakings fine and central spot usually lacking. Song varied, sweet and gurgling, suggesting the purple finch's. Rare summer resident, in open areas near ponds at low and medium elevations.

SWAMP SPARROW   *Melospiza georgiana*

Length 5 inches, dark back, gray breast without streaking. Song a slow trill resembling the junco's. Summer resident, frequent in marshes and on bushy edges of bogs and ponds at low elevations. This bird is most easily identified by its habitat.

white-throated sparrow

song sparrow

Lincoln's sparrow

swamp sparrow

BIRDS

PINE GROSBEAK

Pinicola enucleutor

Length 8 inches, back rosy red, white wing bars. Song a warble resembling that of the purple finch. Winter visitor to coniferous woods on mountain slopes, rarely remaining for the summer.

ROSE-BREASTED GROSBEAK

Pheucticus ludovicianus

Length 7 inches, black and white with rosy breast. Song robinlike but more mellow, call a sharp "keek." Summer resident, frequent in deciduous woods at low elevations. This bird is common in the lowlands and may be seen near the foot of the trail.

EVENING GROSBEAK

Hesperiphona vespertina

Length 7 inches, large beak, conspicuous black, white, and yellow coloration. Song consists of repeated unmusical chirps. Mostly a winter visitor, but occasionally remaining during the summer in open woods and bushy areas at low elevations.

WAXWINGS

The diet of a waxwing is largely fruit (about 90%) and caterpillars, though in late summer it pursues insects as well. The waxwing's crest and black mask are distinctive field marks.

CEDAR WAXWING

Bombycilla cedrorum

Length 6 inches, prominent crest, black mask, yellow band at end of tail. Call a high thin note. Summer resident, frequent in open or bushy areas at low elevations. The cedar waxwing is fond of berries and likely to be found where there is any kind of fruit.

pine grosbeak

rose-breasted grosbeak

evening grosbeak

cedar waxwing

225

WOOD WARBLERS

Wood warblers, generally referred to simply as warblers, are small, active, mostly brightly-colored birds with thin bills. There are a number of species and distinguishing among them is interesting and challenging. The females and immature birds lack the males' vivid coloring and are more difficult to identify. Some people identify warblers by their songs, which takes considerable practice. In spite of the name, the majority of warblers do not warble. Their songs are rather short, often with a definite pattern, and bear a family resemblance. Warblers feed on insects.

BLACK-AND-WHITE WARBLER   *Mniotilta varia*

Length 4½ inches. With the blackpoll, the only warbler that is all black and white, more streaked than the blackpoll. Song a thin high repeated "we-see, we-see" with the second note lower. Summer resident, frequent in woods on lower slopes. Sometimes called the black-and-white creeper, this bird can be recognized by its characteristic habit of moving along the trunk or branch of a tree looking for insects.

TENNESSEE WARBLER   *Vermivora peregrina*

Length 4½ inches, dull-colored bird with a white eye stripe, resembling vireo but with thinner bill and very different song. Song high and in two parts: "zip, zip, zip . . . .zee, zee, zee." Rare summer resident, in deciduous or mixed woods at low and occasionally high elevations. It often sings from the top of a tall tree.

NASHVILLE WARBLER   *Vermivora ruficapilla*

Length 4 inches, bluish-gray head, yellow breast. Song in two parts, the first a series of separate chips and the second a slow trill on a lower pitch. Summer resident, frequent in deciduous and mixed woods from low to high elevations. The Nashville tends to occur at higher elevations than any other warbler except for the blackpoll and myrtle.

PARULA WARBLER   *Parula americana*

Length 4 inches, head bluish, breast yellow with a dark band across it. Song a buzzing trill that drops abruptly at the end. Summer resident, frequent in mixed and coniferous woods at low elevations. It is most likely to be found in moist areas and prefers the luxurious gray usnea lichen for its nest.

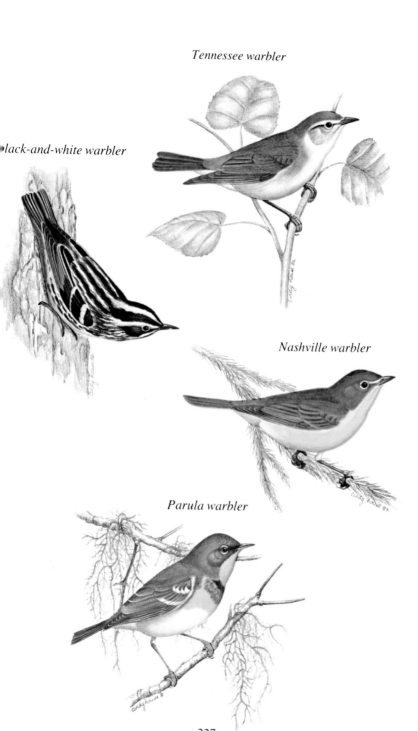

Tennessee warbler

lack-and-white warbler

Nashville warbler

Parula warbler

227

MAGNOLIA WARBLER
Dendroica magnolia

Length 4 inches, brightly colored, yellow breast with black streaks, black face mask, white patches on wings and white tail band. Song a somewhat warbled "weeky, weeky, wicky." Summer resident, common in deciduous and coniferous woods at low and medium elevations. This warbler is easily identified. The song somewhat resembles that of the chestnut-sided warbler, which is not likely to be found in the woods.

CAPE MAY WARBLER
Dendroica tigrina

Length 4 inches. Resembles magnolia warbler but with chestnut cheeks and no white band on tail. Song a high thin repeated "see, see." Summer resident, rare in evergreen woods at low elevations.

YELLOW-RUMPED
or MYRTLE WARBLE
Dendroica coronata

Length 5 inches, yellow shoulder patches and yellow rump. Song a short trill, suggesting a juncos, but rising or falling in pitch. Summer resident, common in woods at low to medium elevations and occasionally in alpine areas. The blackpoll is the only other warbler found as high in the mountains as this one.

BLACK-THROATED GREEN WARBLER
Dendroica virens

Length 4 inches, black throat, conspicuous yellow cheek. Song "zee, zee, zu, zu, zee" or "zee, zee, zee, zu, zee." The "zus" are lower in pitch. Summer resident, frequent in woods at low and medium elevations. This warbler has a distinctive song, one of the easiest to learn. It has been translated as "trees, trees, murm'ring trees."

magnolia warbler

Cape May warbler

yellow-rumped warbler

black-throated green warbler

BLACK-THROATED BLUE WARBLER *Dendroica caerulescens*

Length 4½ inches, black cheek and throat, blue-gray back. Song 2 to 6 shrill nasal "zur, zur" ascending in pitch. Summer resident, frequent in woods at low and medium elevations. The typical song is fairly easy to recognize. There are variations, however, which may be puzzling.

BLACKBURNIAN WARBLER *Dendroica fusca*

Length 4½ inches, bright orange throat, black head markings. Song high and thin notes, "zip, zip, zip, zeee," very high at the end. Summer resident, frequent in woods at low and medium elevations. This brightly colored warbler can be recognized easily even at a considerable distance.

CHESTNUT-SIDED WARBLER *Dendroica pensylvanica*

Length 4½ inches, prominent yellow cap, white breast with chestnut sides. Song a warbled "I wish to see Miss Beecher." Summer resident, frequent in bushy areas on lower slopes. This is a common lowland bird that may be observed near the bottom of the trail at the edges of old fields and thickets.

BAY-BREASTED WARBLER *Dendroica castanea*

Length 5 inches, dark back, chestnut throat. Song a thin high repeated "zee, zee," resembling the song of the Cape May but with the notes tending to run together. Summer resident, infrequent in coniferous woods at low and medium elevations. This bird is likely to be heard in the tops of trees, and is more common in the mountains than the Cape May warbler.

black-throated blue warbler

chestnut-sided warbler

Blackburnian warbler

bay-breasted warbler

231

BIRDS

BLACKPOLL WARBLER
Dendroica striata

Length 4½ inches, black and white with a black cap and white throat. Song a series of high thin "zee, zee" all on one pitch, soft in the beginning, louder in the middle, and softer at the end. Summer resident, common near mountaintops and in the alpine area, occasional in woods on lower slopes. The blackpoll occurs at higher elevations than any other warbler except the myrtle.

OVENBIRD
Seiurus aurocapillus

Length 5 inches, somewhat resembles a small thrush with olive back, but has striped underparts. Song a repeated "teach-er, teacher" becoming increasingly louder and more emphatic. Summer resident, common in woods on lower slopes. This bird is easily recognized by its song. It spends most of its time near the ground, where it builds a well-concealed nest.

WATERTHRUSH
Seiurus noveboracensis

Length 5 inches, resembles ovenbird but with a conspicuous stripe through the eye. Song a loud "quit, quit, quit, chew, chew" dropping at the end. Summer resident, frequent at low elevations near bogs and ponds. The waterthrush spends most of its time on the ground and its behavior resembles that of a sandpiper more than that of a warbler.

YELLOWTHROAT
Geothlypis trichas

Length 4½ inches, prominent yellow throat and breast, black stripe through the eye. Song "witchita, witchita" repeated several times. Summer resident, common at low elevations in open areas and bushy places. Yellowthroats are frequently seen at the foot of trails.

blackpoll warbler

ovenbird

waterthrush

yellowthroat

233

MOURNING WARBLER
Oporornis philadelphia

Length 4½ inches, gray hood encircling head and neck, yellow belly. Song "thur-ree, thur-ree" repeated several times and falling at the end, somewhat similar to the Nashville warbler's. Infrequent summer resident at low elevations. This bird is uncommon throughout the range of this guide. It should be looked for near the foot of the trail, especially in areas that have been recently lumbered.

WILSON'S WARBLER
Wilsonia pusilla

Length 4½ inches, yellow with a black cap. Song a series of chips dropping slightly at the end. Summer resident, rare in bushy or swampy areas at low elevations. This warbler is not often seen but is easy to identify if you can get a good look at it.

CANADA WARBLER
Wilsonia canadensis

Length 5 inches, yellow breast, black necklace across the throat. Song quite varied, a warbled series of notes of which one rendition is "tu, tu, tswee, tu, tu." Summer resident, common in woods at low and medium elevations. This warbler is easier to spot than some of the others, as it frequents bushes or lower branches of trees. The song is distinctive, different from that of any other warbler.

REDSTART
Setophaga ruticilla

Length 4½ inches, male black with orange patches, female gray-brown with yellow patches. Song "che, che, che, che-pa" with the last note lower. Summer resident, common in woods and thickets at low elevations. The redstart has a number of different songs which can be puzzling. However, it spends much of its time near the ground, and its bright coloration makes it fairly easy to spot.

mourning warbler

Wilson's warbler

Canada warbler

redstart

BIRDS

BLACKBIRDS

Blackbirds include the Baltimore oriole and other colorful birds. The only ones that occur in the mountains are black and are much smaller than a crow.

REDWING
or RED-WINGED BLACKBIRD
Agelius phoeniceus

Length 7 inches, black with a white-bordered red patch on the wing. Song a gurgling "konk-a-ree." Summer resident, common near bogs and ponds bordered by marsh or shrubs at low elevations. Redwings nest in low shrubs, sedges, or similar plants.

RUSTY BLACKBIRD
Euphagus carolinus

Length 8 inches, the size of a robin, black with a white eye. Song a high squeaky "ku-a-lee." Summer resident, uncommon near ponds at low, medium, and occasionally high elevations. This bird resembles the grackle but is smaller and does not have a wedge-shaped tail. It generally occurs at higher elevations than the redwing.

GRACKLE
or PURPLE GRACKLE
Quiscalus quiscala

Length 10 to 13 inches, all black with a wedge-shaped tail evident in flight. Song a rasping ascending squeak. Summer resident, frequent in open woods or near water at low elevations. This bird is common in farmlands and may be seen near the foot of trails.

TANAGERS

The vivid color of this thrush-sized bird makes it unmistakable. Only one tanager is found in eastern mountains.

SCARLET TANAGER
Piranga olivacea

Length 6 inches, scarlet with black wings and tail. Song 3 to 6 robin-like phrases but nasal, call a "chip-chur." Summer resident, frequent in deciduous woods at low elevations. It spends most of its time in the tops of tall leafy trees and will likely be noticed by its song.

redwing

rusty blackbird

grackle

scarlet tanager

237

Mammals

There are many mammals in the mountains, but only a few of them are likely to be seen. Most are shy and take cover when humans approach, and some of the smaller species, such as mice and shrews, can only be identified by close examination, which requires trapping. But even though seeing mammals is ultimately a matter of luck, you can derive pleasure from knowing they are part of the mountain environment.

Sightings aside, signs of animal habitation are abundant. Tracks can often be found in mud or on wet ground, and droppings, known as scats, are also common. These are best identified by reference to a field guide dealing specifically with tracks and scats.

Look for evidence of browsing or gnawing. Gnawed tree twigs bespeak deer's winter search for food, and felled trees surrounded by wood chips are unmistakable signs of beaver activity. Some mammals' homes are easy to spot: the squirrel's leafy nest high in a treetop, and the beaver's great mud and branch abode in a pond.

Mammals' calls are difficult to describe, but are a good means of identification. An attempt has been made to approximate those calls you might hear.

Organization

With few exceptions, the mammals in this guide are arranged in order of increasing size — from the tiny brown bat (the only mammal that has true flight) to the mighty moose and bear. Several families are well represented: shrews, weasels, and rodents.

Entries

Each entry includes information on size, distinctive coloring and markings, and habitat. A separate paragraph provides additional notes on diet, habits, and interesting physical adaptations for survival.

MAMMALS

LITTLE BROWN BAT   *Myotis lucifugus*

The only mammal that has true flight. Nocturnal, can be observed at dusk and throughout the night. Resembles a small bird but dodging and twisting flight is distinctive. Occasional on lower slopes of mountains near buildings, caves, or hollow trees, where it sleeps during the daytime.

A bat's wings are membranes that extend between the fingers, somewhat like the webbed feet of a duck, only thinner and much more developed. The bat feeds on insects, making sharp turns in the air with more agility than most birds. It has eyes and can see moderately well, but at night it emits ultrasonic cries and guides itself by the echoes bouncing off solid objects.

HAIRY-TAILED MOLE   *Parascalops breweri*

Small mammal about 5 inches long, tail 1 inch, fur slate-colored. Shovellike front feet and small eyes nearly covered with fur. Resembles a mouse but has no gnawing teeth. Occasional on lower slopes in good soil.

The mole is built for digging and spends most of its life underground, or under litter and fallen logs. It feeds on insects, worms, and some vegetable matter.

STAR-NOSED MOLE   *Condylura cristata*

Similar to the hairy-tailed mole but with fingerlike fleshy projections on its nose. The star-nosed mole prefers low wet ground near streams or lakes, and is a good swimmer. It is more common than the hairy-tailed mole.

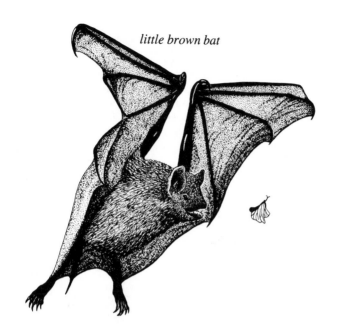

little brown bat

hairy-tailed mole

star-nosed mole

SHREWS

Shrews are small mouse-sized mammals with ears concealed in soft fur, beady eyes, and pointed noses. They are carniverous and have sharp teeth. Every day they must have food equal to their own weight in order to survive. It is easy to identify a shrew but difficult to distinguish among the six species that are found in the mountains, which are mostly separated by technical differences. The habitat and distribution of shrews is largely known as a result of trapping them.

SMOKY SHREW   *Sorex fumeus*

Length 3 inches, tail 2 inches, fur grayish-brown. Common in coniferous or mixed forests, especially where there is a moist layer of leaf mold or other ground vegetation. Occasionally seen above timberline.

LONG-TAILED SHREW   *Sorex dispar*

Resembling smoky shrew but tail longer, up to 2½ inches. Infrequent in cold moist rocky crevices in the mountains at all elevations. This rare shrew was first found in the Adirondacks and later in Tuckerman Ravine on Washington. In old age it loses hair at the end of its tail, the equivalent of baldness in humans.

MASKED SHREW   *Sorex cinereus*

Somewhat less robust than the smoky shrew. Positive identification is made by an examination of its teeth. Frequent in moist forests.

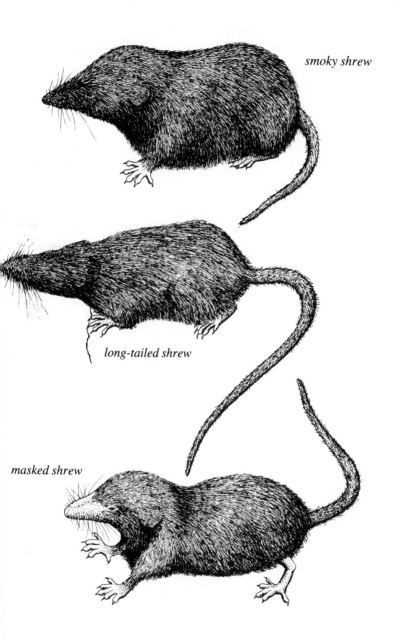

smoky shrew

long-tailed shrew

masked shrew

MAMMALS

WATER SHREW   *Sorex palustris*

A blackish-gray shrew slightly larger than the others. Frequent along borders of ponds and streams at low elevations. It has a stiff fringe of hairs on its hind feet that aid in swimming, and also allow it to run a short distance on the surface of the water.

SHORT-TAILED SHREW   *Blarina brevicauda*

Tail 1 inch long, eyes very small. Frequent in moist woodlands and occasional in the alpine area. This shrew has poisonous saliva which paralyzes small animals.

PIGMY SHREW   *Microsorex hoyi*

About the same length as the other shrews but weighs little more than a dime. Occasional in forests on mountain slopes. This shrew is considered the smallest living mammal. Not much is known about its habits.

water shrew

short-tailed shrew

pigmy shrew

MAMMALS

RODENTS

Rodents are an order of relatively small, gnawing mammals represented in the mountains by the mouse, chipmunk, squirrel, woodchuck, porcupine, and beaver. There are three prevalent species of mice in the mountains: white-footed mice, voles, and lemmings. A number of mice not described here might be found at low elevations.

YELLOW-NOSED or ROCK VOLE   *Microtus chrotorrhinus*

A robust, short-tailed mouse, grayish-brown with a yellow nose, length 2 inches. Occasional in cold moist rock crevices above 3000 feet. In the mountains this vole takes the place of the common lowland meadow mouse. It is seldom seen and much of what is known about it has been obtained by trapping it.

RED-BACKED VOLE   *Clethrionomys gapperi*

Similar to the rock vole but with a brown nose and reddish back, tail 2 inches. Frequent in coniferous, deciduous, or mixed woods, with a preference for damp habitats. It feeds chiefly on vegetable matter and frequently climbs trees.

DEER or WHITE-FOOTED MOUSE   *Peromyscus maniculatus*

White feet, long tail 2 to 5 inches, prominent ears (voles and lemmings have inconspicuous ears). Color from pale grayish-buff to deep reddish-brown, pale to white underneath. Common in forests, open land, and around buildings.

This common mouse is the one most likely to enter camps. It is omniverous, eating many forms of animal and vegetable matter, with a general preference for seeds, nuts, and berries. In the woods it nests in logs, stumps, and trees — taking over an abandoned bird nest — or in any other convenient cavity or hole. The deer mouse is food for a number of predatory mammals and birds.

NORTHERN BOG LEMMING   *Synaptomys borealis*

Resembles a vole but with tail only 1 inch long. Lives in wet alpine and subalpine meadows and heaths, where it makes trails in grasses and sedges. As these habitats are uncommon in the mountains, the lemming is rare.

246

yellow-nosed vole

northern bog lemming

deer mouse

red-backed vole

MAMMALS

EASTERN CHIPMUNK
Tamias striatus

Small mammal about 6 inches long with a bushy tail 4 inches, which is held straight up when it runs. White stripe on side of face and on back. Call a sharp "cuck, cuck, cuck," which is often heard before the animal is seen. Common on lower slopes of mountains in deciduous forests and woody areas.

The chipmunk readily becomes tame and is often seen near buildings. Although it can climb quite well, it spends most of its time on the ground. It makes its nest in a hole in the ground and retreats there when alarmed. It eats seeds, nuts, and berries, and less frequently worms, slugs and large insects.

RED SQUIRREL
Tamiasciurus hudsonicus

Body 8 inches, bushy tail 5 inches, fur yellowish or reddish, pale to white underneath. Spends most of its time in trees, often noticed by its call, a "cher, cher." Common in coniferous or mixed forests and in swampy woods.

The red squirrel is more likely to be seen in the mountains than any other mammal. When an intruder enters its territory it flies into a rage. Its call becomes noisier, and it stamps its feet and flicks its tail while remaining safely on the branch of a tree. If approached closely it moves higher up the tree but its noise does not subside until the intruder has left. The squirrel eats a variety of seeds, fruits, and mushrooms, which it stores in a tree or in a sheltered place on the ground. Its nest, a large mass of leaves, moss, and ground litter, rests in a hollow tree in a cluster of branches.

WOODCHUCK
or GROUNDHOG
Marmota monax

Yellowish-brown to brown mammal 18 to 25 inches long with a tail 6 inches. Heavy-bodied and not a fast runner, usually retreating to its hole when people approach. Occasionally emits a low whistle. Common in fields and bushy areas, occasional in open woods and in the alpine area where there is enough soil to dig a hole.

The woodchuck lives in a hole in the ground — often a tunnel with several entrances — and seldom goes more than 100 yards from its home. Although not as fleet as most mammals, it can run faster than a man for a short distance. It feeds mostly on grass, leaves, and flowers, and occasionally on fruits and tree bark. The woodchuck hibernates through the winter, not emerging from its hole till early spring.

red squirrel

eastern chipmunk

woodchuck

249

PORCUPINE

Erethizon dorsatum

A heavy-bodied, short-legged mammal about 20 inches long with an 8 inch tail. Fur dark brown to black with some white-tipped hairs. Quills prominent, barbed, up to 5 inches long, white with black tips. Call a series of grunts, groans, and high-pitched cries. Frequent on wooded slopes and around camps.

The porcupine feeds mainly on bark — killing trees by completely girdling them — and occasionally on fruit. In winter it eats the tips of conifer branches. It is fond of salt and will chew anything that has salt on it. The procupine's den is a crevice in a ledge or under rocks, littered with brown fecal pellets. Contrary to a common misconception, the porcupine cannot throw its quills but rather slaps its tail quickly into the face of an unwary dog or other animal.

BEAVER

Castor canadensis

Aquatic mammal 30 inches long, tail 10 inches, horizontally flattened and scaly, fur heavy and rich brown. Frequent in streams and lakes on the lower slopes and occasionally ascending to alpine ravines.

Beaver activity is readily recognized by a dam or series of dams in a pond, with a system of connecting waterways and canals. The dam is constructed of branches, stones, and mud, and old ones are often overgrown with vegetation and strong enough to hold a human. Behind the dam there is usually a beaver house made of the same materials and measuring up to 6 feet high. The beaver is nocturnal, venturing forth in late afternoon. It slaps the water loudly with its tail when diving. Beavers love bark and gnaw down trees up to 1 foot in diameter to obtain this favorite food. They prefer poplar and alder but will eat other hardwoods.

porcupine

beaver

MAMMALS

WEASELS

Weasels are a family of small, active, carniverous mammals whose members include the mink, marten, fisher, and skunk.

SHORT-TAILED WEASEL   *Mustela erminea*

Small slender mammal up to 9 inches long with tail 4 inches. Fur brown with white feet and underparts, all white in winter. Frequent in brushy or wooded areas but not often seen.

The weasel has sharp canine teeth and can kill animals several times its size. It eats moles, shrews, mice (which it pursues into holes), chipmunks, and occasionally a rabbit. The weasel spends most of its time on the ground but can climb trees. It is bold and curious. When it sees a person, it does not flee but darts in and out of cover watching closely.

MINK   *Mustela vison*

Larger than a weasel, up to 17 inches, tail 8 inches, fur dark brown. Occasional near streams and ponds on lower mountain slopes.

The mink eats a variety of small mammals and fish. A good swimmer, it spends much of its time in the water and will travel considerable distances overland to locate another stream. Its footprints on muddy banks are nearly round, about 1¼ inches in diameter, with small claw marks.

MARTEN   *Martes americana*

Body 17 inches, tail 9 inches. Resembles a mink but with yellow-brown fur shading to dark brown on tail and legs, pale buff patch on throat and breast. Generally rare, in coniferous forests on mountain slopes, but somewhat more common in Maine.

The marten is a good climber and pursues its favorite food, the red squirrel, to the tops of trees. It eats other small mammals when they are available and does some of its hunting on the ground. The marten is so rare that the sight of one in the woods would probably be a once-in-a-lifetime event.

short-tailed weasel

mink

marten

253

MAMMALS

SKUNK
Mephitis mephitis

Body 15-18 inches, tail 9 inches, fur black with two white stripes on its back which join at its head. Often detected by odor. Occasional in the mountains in open areas and around campsites.

The skunk is a slow-moving animal with no need to hurry — its defense an odorous spray which it discharges from glands under its tail. If a skunk stamps its feet and raises its tail it is about to discharge, but it will not do so unless it is annoyed or cornered. The skunk eats mice and other small mammals when it can catch them, but feeds mostly on insects and wild fruits. Although not normally attacked by other animals, it may become the prey of a bobcat, fox, or owl during a harsh winter.

FISHER
Martes pennanti

Body up to 25 inches, tail 14 inches, fur dark brown to nearly black, most of the hairs white-tipped. Frequent in hardwoods and mixed woods but not often seen.

The fisher is the largest and most powerful member of the weasel family in the Northeast. In spite of its name it does not fish, but is not averse to eating a dead fish if it finds one. It eats a variety of mammals varying in size from mouse to beaver. The fisher is one of the few mammals that can kill a porcupine, turning the prickly prey over with a flash of a paw and ripping open the soft underbelly. In winter, porcupines are an important source of food for the fisher.

VARYING HARE
or SNOWSHOE RABBIT
Lepus americanus

Body 13 to 18 inches, tail 1 inch and inconspicuous, prominent ears 3 inches, fur brown. When startled, runs in leaps measuring up to 10 feet. Common on mountain slopes in thickets and forests.

The hare is a vegetarian and feeds on grass, leaves of various herbs, buds, and twigs. It cannot dig but takes shelter under a log or in an abandoned hole. When resting it is difficult to see, with ears folded and head drawn into the body. Its small round brown fecal droppings may be seen in its path. In winter the hare turns white, develops coarse hairs on its feet that are the "snowshoes," and eats twigs, buds, and bark, occasionally girdling trees.

skunk

fisher

varying hare

MAMMALS

RACCOON

Procyon lotor

Body 18-28 inches, tail 8 to 12 inches, fur grayish-brown with a black face mask and black rings on the tail. Common in the lowlands, occasional in the mountains around campsites, ponds, and streams.

The raccoon is a good fighter and has strong teeth. It is omnivorous, eating frogs, fish, crayfish, mice, fruits, nuts, and seeds. If near water it washes its food before eating it, though the reason for this is not clear. The raccoon is primarily nocturnal and, while a good climber, spends most of the time on the ground. Its footprints impressed in mud are about 3 inches long with prominent long toes.

RED FOX

Vulpes fulva

Body 2 feet, tail 15 inches, fur reddish-yellow, tail bushy with a white tip, appearance of a small dog. Occasional in mountains near the edge of the forest or in open country.

The fox is a common lowland mammal that may wander up the lower slopes of mountains. Its diet is varied. An omnivore, it eats mice and other small mammals, some insects, wild fruits, and a small amount of grass. When hunting it goes at a slow trot. If alarmed it will flee at top speed.

BOBCAT
or WILDCAT

Lynx rufus

A large cat up to 30 inches long, short tail about 5 inches, short ear tufts up to 1 inch. Fur brownish with darker spots. Uncommon in forests on mountain slopes.

Active at night, the bobcat is secretive, quietly retreating upon the arrival of an intruder. Although it can climb trees it spends most of its time on the ground. The snowshoe rabbit is a favorite food, but it eats many other mammals, including an occasional porcupine and sick or wounded deer. It makes a home for its young in caves on ledges and sometimes in the shelter of the stump of a fallen tree.

raccoon

red fox

bobcat

LYNX

Lynx canadensis

The lynx resembles the bobcat but is larger, with longer ear tufts, bigger feet, fur paler and spots less conspicuous. The short tail has a completely black tip. Rare in forests, mostly at high elevations.

The lynx is shy and almost entirely nocturnal. It has large eyes and can see well in dim light; hence the expression "lynx-eyed." Its diet is similar to the bobcat's. In winter the lynx's large feet act as snowshoes and it feeds mainly on snowshoe rabbits. Its den is in a cave or under a stump.

EASTERN COYOTE

Canis latrans

Body 3 feet, tail 1 foot, fur gray or reddish-gray with rusty legs. Resembles a dog of the collie type but coloration different, nose more pointed and tail held down when running. Occasional on lower slopes in bush country, sometimes ascending to higher elevations. Call a series of high-pitched yaps.

The eastern coyote belongs to the same species as the western coyote but is of a different race. It is carniverous and feeds mainly on sizable mammals, though it will only rarely attack a deer. A dog-like track seen far from a building or trail is probably the coyote's. Coyotes sometimes mate with dogs giving rise to "coy-dogs," but the offspring is not likely to persist in the wild.

WHITE-TAILED DEER

Odocoileus virginianus

About 3 feet high, 4 to 6 feet long, reddish coat, tail 1 foot with white underside, wagging and conspicuous when the deer is running. Male has antlers. Frequent in forests and open areas on mountain slopes.

Deer eat grass, flowers, buds, and twigs. A buck tends to stay in the same area for days, and often makes trails which can be followed for a short distance. Its hoof is cleft and the print is up to 3 inches long. It sheds its antlers in early spring but soon grows a new set. The fawns are spotted and will lie motionless when an intruder is in the area. In winter deer eat twigs and branches.

lynx

eastern coyote

white-tailed deer

MOOSE
Alces alces

A large dark brown mammal up to 6 feet high with overhanging snout and "bell" on its throat. Antlers with large flat area and several prongs. An erratic wanderer in forests found near marshes and ponds, more common in the northern parts of Maine, especially in the Katahdin area.

Whereas deer are timid and flee as soon as they see a man, moose simply wander off. The moose eats grass, sedge, buds, and twigs. It is an excellent swimmer and readily enters ponds to feed on water lilies and other aquatic plants. In the rutting season, a bull moose is not afraid of man; in fact, it is advisable to give the bull a wide berth. Moose tracks resemble deer tracks but the prints are much larger, about 6 inches long.

BLACK BEAR
Ursus americanus

Body 5 to 6 feet long, height 2 to 3 feet, ears short, tail inconspicuous. Frequent in hardwood and mixed forests, and in lumbered areas on mountain slopes.

Seeing a bear in the woods is an exciting event. Occasionally they are spotted in trees but more often seen on the ground, lumbering off through the woods. Although the bear is fond of meat, it is too clumsy to catch most mammals. It does dig mice and other small mammals out of the ground, and pull apart stumps to get ants. It eats some grass, sedge, and various fruits and nuts, being particularly fond of beechnuts, which it gathers from platforms it builds in the branches of trees. Claw marks can often be seen on beech trees. The bear is a powerful animal. It is not known to attack people in the woods, but bears that feed at dumps should not be closely approached.

moose

black bear

Cold-Blooded Vertebrates

Cold-blooded vertebrates are animals whose body temperatures vary with that of the external environment. They hibernate or become torpid in the winter, and you are not likely to see them in the mountains when temperatures are low.

Organization

There are three classes of cold-blooded vertebrates included in this guide: reptiles, amphibians, and fish. Reptiles include snakes and turtles; toads, frogs, and salamanders are amphibians. Each class is described briefly at the head of its section.

Entries

Each entry indicates size, color, distinctive markings, habitat, and frequency of appearance.

REPTILES

Reptiles breathe air and lay their eggs on land or, in the case of some snakes, bear their young alive. Although some snakes are aggressive if approached closely, poisonous ones do not occur in the mountains.

GARTER SNAKE *Thamnophis sirtalis*

Length 18 to 26 inches, brown with 3 yellowish stripes. Color variable but stripes always evident. Frequent on lower slopes. The garter snake is not poisonous but may bite if handled.

NORTHERN BROWN *Storeria dekayi*
or DEKAY's SNAKE

Length 9 to 13 inches, resembles garter snake but smaller, without stripes. A dark downward streak on each side of the head. Occasional at low elevations, usually in moist places.

RED-BELLIED SNAKE *Storeria occipitomaculata*

Length 8 to 10 inches, brown with red belly and 3 light spots on the back of the head. Occasional in open woods or near bogs at low and medium elevations.

GREEN SNAKE *Opheodrys vernalis*

Length 14 to 20 inches, pale green above and pale beneath. Occasional in open woodlands and open areas at low elevations.

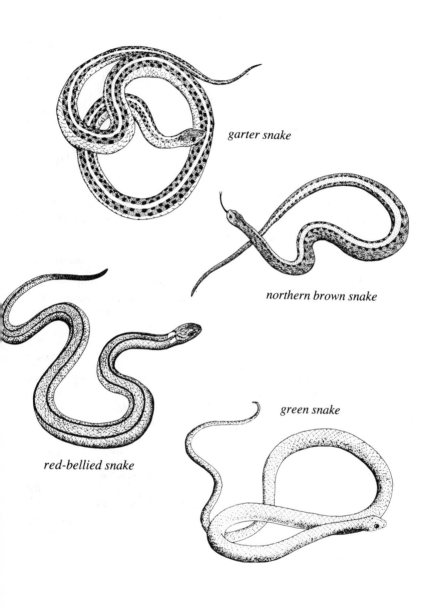

garter snake

northern brown snake

red-bellied snake

green snake

COLD-BLOODED VERTEBRATES

PAINTED TURTLE   *Chrysemys picta*

Length 4 to 6 inches, dark with light horizontal bands across the shell, 2 bright yellow spots on each side of the head. Occasional in ponds at low elevations.

AMPHIBIANS

Amphibians include toads, frogs, and salamanders. They lay their eggs in the water and the young are born as tadpoles. As they mature, they become air breathers and can live on land or in the water. Many salamanders are land dwellers, but require a moist environment like that found under stones or logs. The following descriptions give typical color but there may be considerable variation.

AMERICAN TOAD   *Bufo americanus*

Length 2 to 3 inches, brown to gray with dry warty skin. Frequent in mountain woods up to the tree line. Toads lay their eggs in a pond or temporary pool. Those seen high in the mountains, where there is little water, are presumably unable to breed.

GREEN FROG   *Rana clamitans*

Length 2 to 3½ inches, green or brown, often with dark spots on back, dark cross bands on hind legs. Voice a banjolike "plunk," often repeated several times. Frequent at low elevations in springs, mudholes, small streams, and on edges of ponds.

MINK FROG   *Rana septentrionalis*

Length 2 to 3 inches, resembles green frog but tends to have darker spots and lacks cross bands on hind legs. Voice a rather deep and rapid "cut, cut, cut, cut." Frequent at low to medium elevations, especially at edges of ponds and where lily pads are plentiful. When handled it emits a musky odor resembling that of a mink.

painted turtle

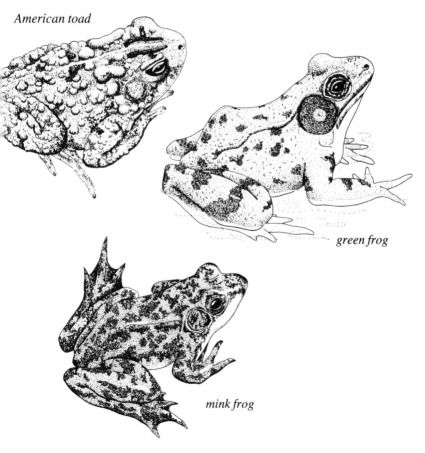

American toad

green frog

mink frog

COLD-BLOODED VERTEBRATES

SPRING PEEPER   *Hyla crucifer*

Length 1 inch, gray or brown with a dark cross on the back. Voice a high piping note repeated at frequent intervals. Frequent in second growth woodlands near water or temporary pools at low elevations. A chorus of spring peepers is a common sound in the spring. The "song" is produced by means of a pouch which is inflated to balloonlike proportions and then deflated. The spring peeper is secretive and seldom seen in summer. It occasionally climbs shrubs or low trees.

GRAY TREE FROG   *Hyla versicolor*
or TREE TOAD

Length 1 to 2 inches, gray with mottled, somewhat warty, back, prominent white spot beneath the eye, adhesive disks at end of the toe. Voice a musical trill. Frequent in the woods near water at low elevations. It often climbs trees, but is difficult to see because it is well camouflaged.

WOOD FROG   *Rana sylvestris*

Length 1½ to 3 inches, pale to dark but always with a prominent dark patch through the eye. Voice a hoarse croaking, suggestive of farm machinery being pulled by a horse. Frequent in woods at low elevations. The wood frog is the first to sing in the spring, but sings only for a week or two.

spring peeper

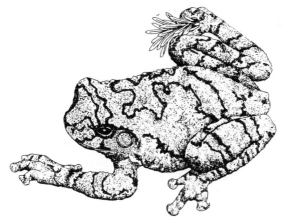

gray tree frog

wood frog

SPRING
or PURPLE SALAMANDER
Gyrinophilus porphyriticus

Length 5 to 7 inches, brownish-pink to reddish with some dark markings, giving a generally cloudy appearance, dark line from head to nostril. Young in water have branched gills on both sides of the head. Occasional in springs, streams, or wet forests at low elevations.

SPOTTED SALAMANDER
Ambystoma maculatum

Length 6 to 7½ inches, black to bluish-black with pale spots in an irregular row on the back. Occasional in ponds or wet woods at low elevations.

RED-SPOTTED NEWT
or RED EFT
Nothophthalamus viridescens

Length 3 to 4 inches. Aquatic stage olive-green, tail yellowish with black spots; land stage bright to dull red or orange. Common in ponds and streams and on the forest floor on low and medium slopes. This is the salamander most likely to be seen in the mountains.

RED-BACKED SALAMANDER
Plethodon cinereus

Length 2 to 3½ inches. Red phase, a red stripe from head to tail bordered with dark band; lead phase, dark gray to black with white underparts. Frequent in wooded areas on low and medium slopes. Considered to be the most common salamander, but as it usually hides it is not often seen.

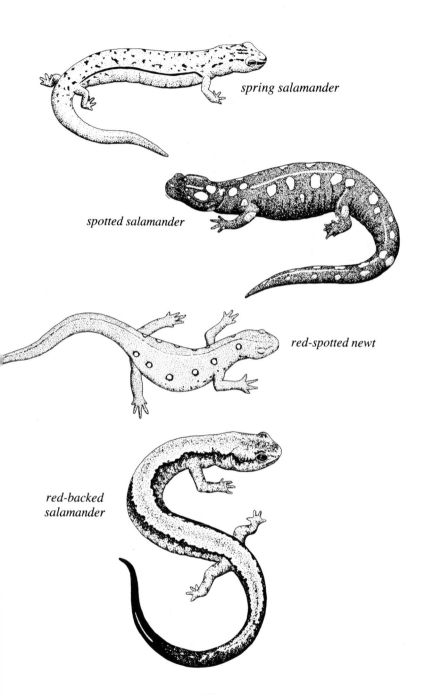

spring salamander

spotted salamander

red-spotted newt

red-backed
salamander

COLD-BLOODED VERTEBRATES

DUSKY SALAMANDER   *Desmognathus fuscus*

Length 2½ to 4½ inches, gray or brown with a light strip from eye to angle of jaw, keeled tail. Occasional on low and medium slopes along edges of woodland streams, never far from water.

TWO-LINED SALAMANDER   *Eurycea bislineata*

Length 2½ to 4 inches, yellow belly with a dark stripe from head to tail. Occasional along brooks on low and medium slopes, in warm weather wandering far into the forest.

FISH

Fish are scarce in the mountains because streams are small and temperatures in mountain lakes low.

BROOK TROUT   *Salvelinus fontinalis*

Length 3 to 7 inches, larger in the lowlands, olive-green to bluish-green with light yellow spots on sides. Common in larger mountain streams. The trout is native but lowland streams are usually stocked. It works its way up small streams until stopped by waterfalls or dwindling water.

SLIMY SCULPIN   *Cottus cognatus*

Length 2 to 3 inches, flattened head, mottled brown to gray, weak spines on some of the fins. Frequent in mountain streams at low and medium elevations. It is found chiefly under stones in rock-bottomed, clear streams.

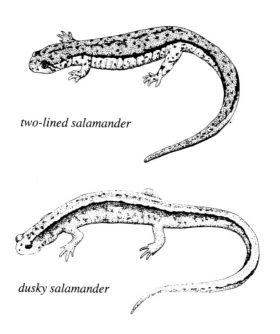

two-lined salamander

dusky salamander

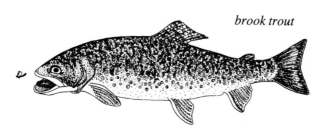

brook trout

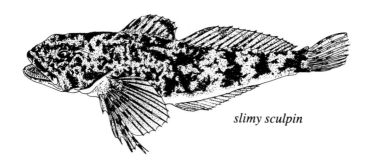

slimy sculpin

Index

INDEX

INDEX

INDEX

281

INDEX

INDEX